Letters from
the Coun

Letters from Across the Country

Marsha Boulton

McArthur & Company

Canadian Cataloguing in Publication Data

  Boulton, Marsha
    Letters from across the country

  ISBN 1-55278-098-8

  1. Farm life — Ontario — Anecdotes. I. Title.

  S522.C3B677 1999   630'.9713   C99-931749-0

Composition and Design by *Michael P. Callaghan*
Typeset at *Moons of Jupiter* (Toronto)
Cover Design by *Tania Craan*
Cover Photographs by *John Reeves*
Printed in Canada by *Transcontinental Printing* (Quebec)

McArthur & Company
322 King Street West, Suite 402
Toronto, ON, M5V 1J2

10 9 8 7 6 5 4 3 2 1

Table of Contents

FOREWORD AND ACKNOWLEDGEMENTS

Mrs. Drinkwater found me in the garden on a bright summer day. After reading the original *Letters from the Country*, she had an approximate idea of my co-ordinates. But the postmistress would not tell her exactly where the farm was and the municipal office was "mum's the word." Willfully undeterred, my personal Miss Marple deduced that I had probably been sent flowers at some point in my 20 years on the farm.

She found me through the florist.

"I'm so glad it's not one of those 'everything-is-new farms,'" Mrs. Drinkwater said while I walked her around the farm.

That it is not, as the photographs in this third volume of "letters" should illustrate. My thanks for these images go to photographer John Reeves and visual artist Michael Callaghan, along with friends, relatives and my constant companion and fellow wordsmith, Stephen "Moose" Williams.

Over the years, many readers have written to me with their stories about "the crazy lady with the sheep who lives down the road." There seems to be one on every concession.

Many of these letters have been remembrances of favourite animals ranging from a milk-drinking horse to "Bubbles the Killer Cow," who would defend her calf at all costs. Somewhere out there lives a pair of hens who made the trek from a farm in North Bay all the way down to suburban Mississauga in the undercarriage of a pickup. Thanks to all of you for sharing — with the greatest of affection — your memories and your tribulations.

This book incorporates many of those stories, constructed, combined and construed as I envision them. Many names and places are fact, others are up for the guessing.

Somewhere in this book I say that "E-mail and voice mail have yet to replace real mail." I hope that is true, although the former are becoming awfully convenient. Please keep those cards and letters coming. They are always an inspiration.

The farm has always been a form of sanctuary for me. I thank the Writers' Development Trust for assisting me in maintaining that equilibrium.

My bold new Canadian publisher, McArthur & Company, under the guiding hand of my affably exuberant friend Kim McArthur, have offered support and good cheer throughout. You can't sink a rainbow.

Lately, Wally the Wonder Dog has tended to steal the show at public appearances I have made with the CBC Radio program *Fresh Air*. He's the clown in the dog suit on the cover of this book. My thanks to *Fresh Air* host, Jeff Goodes, and the hundreds of people who assemble the show, for putting up with the antics.

It takes a lot of character to survive life with "the crazy lady with the sheep." I am fortunate to have found that character in my beloved Moose.

And god bless you Mrs. Drinkwater.

Spring

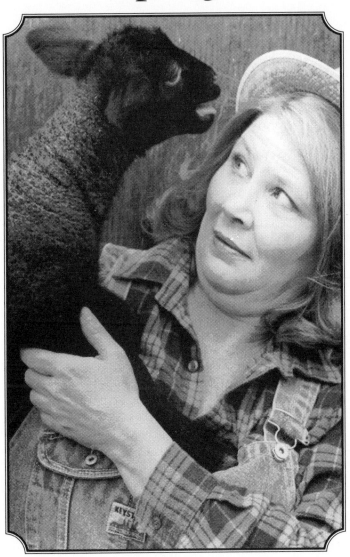

CHICKEN SOUP
FOR THE CHICKEN'S SOUL

Of all farm animals, the lowly chicken is the least likely of creatures to draw its caretaker into the sort of personal bond that can develop between a goatherd and a favourite nanny, or a swineherd and a lovable old boar.

The words "chicken" and "personality" are seldom seen in close proximity. However, occasionally one bird will rise above the rest and display a willful temperament that distinguishes it from the others. Such can be said of certain roosters who will crow back at you when you feel like crowing yourself.

Of course, this is the sort of behaviour one keeps to oneself. It can be highly humiliating to have a neighbour drop by and catch you out in the barn crowing with the roosters. I know this to be true.

Chickens tend to be helpless creatures, viewed largely as economic units and raised in confined situations designed to maximize production. Those of us who cast monetary considerations to the wind, and pamper our chickens with things such as leg room and natural light, generally suffer some unexpected consequences.

One summer I raised 100 chicks from day-olds to six-week-olds, which is adolescence in terms of chickens. At that stage, I allowed them to range freely in the field behind their coop, where they could forage for bugs and greenery to supplement their grain-fed diet.

Moose and I felt confident enough to leave them alone one sunny afternoon when we went off to an auction in search of 50-cent lots of nuts and bolts and other treasures. While we were gone, storm clouds gathered squarely over the farm, suddenly depositing what must have been a wall of water.

On our return, we galloped across the muddy field to the coop and found the range full of sodden chickens lying like saturated feather pillows in the mud. Instead of retreating to their straw-dry coop, the young idiots had stayed out in the rain. Worse, they had apparently tried to swallow the deluge.

From the tense, skyward projection of certain of their legs, some of them were definitely past-tense chickens. But many were still gurgling.

Hauling them into the coop, Moose and I rubbed them with straw. Their eyes were vacant black holes; scrawny necks twisted back over clammy feathers glued to bony breasts. I was ready to give up when the Moose decided that what they needed was a stiff drink.

Separating Moose from his vodka is not something that occurs every day. I am not even allowed to sip a martini, it having been determined years ago that such rocket fuel is "too spicy" for my delicate constitution. But in this life-or-death situation, Moose became the soul of generosity. While I tended the sputtering flock, he fetched the freezer-cold Stolichnaya.

Finding the vodka was no problem, but the eyedropper eluded him. Instead, Moose brought with him the smallest spoon he could find — the slightly tarnished, sterling silver baby spoon my godmother gave me.

I cradled one of the birds, forcing its beak ajar, and Moose carefully measured a tiny quantity of spirits into the spoon. We didn't hear the creature gulp, but its eyes did flash wide open as the refined Russian potato mash slid down its gullet. The chicken began jerking weakly, cocking its head and blinking. When we set the pathetic thing back onto the straw, it stayed upright.

"It works," exclaimed Moose. "If chickens had lips, he'd be smacking them."

And so it went.

Two hours and twenty-six ounces later, the doused and soused survivors were back to preening and clucking as though nothing had happened.

For the longest time, I thought that Moose and I might be alone in the invocation of extreme measures involving alcohol and chickens. But as in everything associated with farming, once the story is out, someone else has already been there.

For Sandy, a genteel chicken-keep who lives at Farmer's Walk farm in the Hockley Valley north of Toronto, it all started with a rooster named Clarence.

Clarence was a barred-rock cockerel in the bloom of youth when he arrived at Sandy's henhouse with his mate Mabel in tow. The henhouse was heaven on earth to Clarence. Sandy called it "The University Women's Club," much to the dismay of her upstanding aunt who had been a member of the real thing.

Clarence slept beside Mabel faithfully every night but came the dawn and he was up and crowing, ready to make his amorous rounds. Sandy noted the wear and tear on the hens, particularly her favourite, a plump red-feathered bird named Henny Penny.

"Henny Penny went tits up one day because Clarence wore her out," Sandy told me. Thereafter, she determined that: "Roosters should not live with hens." With that pronouncement, Sandy was halfway up the poultry learning curve.

A crisis arose one day when she found Clarence leaning against the side of the henhouse looking decidedly unwell.

By then, Sandy knew that a sick chicken in the morning would be a dead chicken by noon. Panicked, she called Anson, her neighbourhood chicken expert, and he arrived with his wife's baby thermometer to check Clarence's vital signs. The message, according to the mercury, was that Clarence was almost a broiler.

Although the stockpot was the obvious solution to Clarence's dilemma, Sandy refused to accept the prognosis without pursuing all options. While Anson watched in wonderment, she bundled Clarence into her car and took him to the veterinarian.

The vet took one look at Clarence and promptly declared that she was not a chicken vet. However, Sandy was adamant. In the examining room, Clarence was once again subjected to the indignity of the thermometer. The formal diagnosis was that Clarence was "a very sick bird." The vet gave him a shot of antibiotics and provided a small jug of medicine which was to be administered with an eyedropper.

Thirty-seven dollars later, Sandy and Clarence were free to leave.

Back at Farmer's Walk, Sandy struggled to treat the squirming rooster. She secured Clarence under her arm and held his rubbery wattles to immobilize him. After three tries, she got the eyedropper into Clarence's beak.

Then disaster struck. Clarence shook his head abruptly and swallowed the tip of the eyedropper in the process.

Horrified, Sandy again bundled the rooster into the car and sped back to the vet's.

After Sandy explained the circumstance, the vet examined Clarence again and announced that retrieval of the foreign object would involve a surgical inter-vention approximating evisceration and a procedural fee of $150.

Since the initial curative investment of $37 was arguably ten times the market value of past-his-prime Clarence, Sandy decided to see if the old bird could get along with an eyedropper nib somewhere in the works.

Clarence lived out his days shaking his head fre-quently as if trying to dislodge something in his throat. His crow was more of a disjointed *ack ack ack* than *cock-a-doodle-do*. Otherwise, he thrived as the cock of Farmer's Walk.

The rooster was ill toward the end of his life, but Sandy eschewed the vet this time. Like Moose, she put her faith in the bottle. Accordingly, Sandy told me that Clarence "became something of an alcoholic," but he did not appear to suffer.

Fortunately, Sandy's husband was an airline pilot who could avail himself of the miracle of duty-free shopping, as well as those perfectly chicken-sized air-line booze mini-bottles. Thus, Clarence was able to consume the best whiskey money could buy as he made his gradual march to the great single-malt-maker in the sky.

Between Dr. Moose's Miracle Vodka Cure and Sandy's Whiskey Poultry Hospice, perhaps extreme measures involving poultry and alcohol are not as uncommon as I thought. Even the lowly, lipless chicken can benefit from an occasional cup of good cheer.

HAPPY TRAILS, "SADDLE PARDNER"

When I heard the news that the King of the Cowboys, Roy Rogers, had died, I took it hard.

The first letter that I ever wrote to anyone was to Roy Rogers.

I was five years old and I had been a Roy Rogers fan from the first moment that the black and white television flickered to life in the suburban living room where I grew up in the fifties.

Those were the days when television was a kind of a miracle and watching anything on it was a special event. I would spend half an hour just getting dressed to watch *The Roy Rogers Show*. It was the polite thing to do. (Heck, the lady who lived next door used to say "excuse me" to her television whenever she left the room.)

I wore a white straw cowboy hat, strapped firmly under my chin with an elastic of sorts. And I tied a plaid kerchief at my neck above a red-checkered western shirt that had silver buttons shaped like horseshoes. They didn't make designer blue-jeans for kids in those days, so I wore regular blue pants that my mother made into regulation cowboy chaps by adding a strip of leather fringe down the side.

My cowboy boots might have looked like plain old puddle jumpers, but they had tinfoil covering the toes. Around my waist I wore a holster with two plastic six-shooters capable of delivering a payload of water in any direction for about three feet.

Before the show started, my parents would move my rocking horse in front of the TV screen. It was a pink rocking horse that bounced on springs, but while I watched Roy Rogers it was transformed into a golden stallion who would rear at my will and gallop after any bad guys that dared stray into the living room.

Six-guns might blaze, but I don't remember seeing any blood or ever being afraid that the good guys wouldn't win. In fact, the only thing I remember ever being mortally wounded on *The Roy Rogers Show* were the rubber tires on Nellybelle, Roy's ranch jeep. And that was just fine with me because the Old West wasn't about jeeps, it was about horses and chuckwagons and herding cows named doggies. It was Cole Porter for goodness sakes, and Roy singing: "Oh give me land, lots of land, Under starry skies above, Don't fence me in . . ."

In all of the years that I spent watching the adventures of Roy Rogers and Dale Evans on the Double R-Bar Ranch, it never occurred to me that they were both older than my parents. It never occurred to me that they were a childless couple living in the middle of a post-war baby boom. Dale ran a diner, but the only help Roy ever gave her seemed to involve testing her pies. And even though they always rode happily into the sunset together, Roy saved his kisses for Trigger. Weird, but it helped me to establish some priorities.

For instance, after watching *The Roy Rogers Show,* I never wanted to be a cowgirl because it was obvious that cowboys got the best horses.

The Lone Ranger had Silver.

The Cisco Kid had Diabolo.

Gene Autry had Champion, and Hopalong Cassidy had Topper — but surely the best horse was Trigger.

Girls usually rode nameless brown horses. Sure Dale's little buckskin gelding Buttermilk was a nice horse, but nothing compared to Trigger who could run like the wind and untie knots with his teeth.

So when Nestle's Quick announced a contest that involved kids writing in with the name for a palomino pony that was the spitting miniature of Trigger — I was there. The kid who came up with the best name would win the pony.

I remember wracking my brain for days. It was all I could think about. My mother read the rules and told me that the contest was only open to American kids, but I was sure that couldn't be true.

Roy Rogers would never deny his Canadian "pard-ners."

As long as we took good care of animals, and treated other kids and old people right, we were all "saddle pals" according to the Code of the West.

It took me two days to write the letter. Painstaking writing, just to keep all of the letters between the lines I had drawn with my ruler.

When I was done, I gave it to my mother to mail. And I waited. I waited for months and months. But I never got a reply.

Around that time, I gave up on cowboys and contests.

Years later, when I was a teenager, we were on a family trip in California. Crossing a scrubby waste-land where the tumbleweed was real, we came to a kind of middle-class oasis known as Apple Valley — home of Roy Rogers and Dale Evans and their museum.

We stopped.

America is full of kitsch disguised as museums, and this was no exception. It had everything from Dale's square-dance dresses, encased in glass, to every saddle Roy ever sat in and every guitar "The Singing Cowboy" ever held.

But the shrine was surely the critters — or at least their preciously preserved remains.

Poised against a painted western panorama there was Bullet the Wonder Dog — Roy and Dale's faithful

Spring

German Shepherd — standing next to Dale's horse, Buttermilk, still as plain as plain, despite his red saddle and trimmings.

The *pièce de résistance* was Trigger — the real Trigger — the half-thoroughbred palomino foaled in 1933 and originally named Golden Cloud — The Smartest Horse in the West — Roy's co-star in more that 180 television show and movies — the horse he fell in love with in 1939 and bought for the princely sum of $2,500 with his own money when the studio wouldn't pony up the dough.

Trigger was mounted in that famous rearing pose of his, wearing his black and silver parade saddle with the solid silver saddle horn that would have given any cowboy pause on a hot day.

He looked frozen. He looked so real that he was unreal. He certainly did not look anything like a 33-year-old horse, which is what he was when he died in 1965. For crying out loud, when I was watching *The Roy Rogers Show*, Trigger was old enough to be my father. And just seeing him there, breathless but forever golden, made me want to cry out loud. Further back in the exhibit, Trigger Jr. — no relation — was stuffed. I looked around, but there was no sign of the Nestle's Quick pony.

The museum had everything and anything you ever wanted to know about Roy and Dale and their private lives, their marriages, their children, their tragedies and their Christianity. They were human. Roy wasn't even really Roy — he was Leonard Franklin Slye, born in Cincinnati and raised in Duck Run, Ohio. He had never been a real cowboy.

On the way out, there was the inevitable souvenir shop, filled with postcards and paper weights, cowboy hats and string neckties. Something about the whole experience disturbed me terribly. Right beside the cash register there was a wicker basket filled with cellophane-wrapped, fossilized Trigger droppings. For sale.

I left without any souvenir. The museum folks said Roy and Dale often stopped by the museum, but it just wasn't our lucky day. Besides, I don't know what I would have said to a hero who didn't have the good manners to write a letter back to a little "pardner."

Decades afterward, I still harboured a childish hurt in my heart over Roy Rogers and my failed entry in the Nestle's Quick contest.

Then, last summer, my mother visited the farm and brought with her one of those inevitable bags full of "stuff" that mothers always show up with. Stuff she has been "keeping for you" for years. Stuff she finds while cleaning out a drawer that she's cleaned out 20 times before.

One of the things she brought me was the letter that I wrote to Roy Rogers. She never did mail it.

Dear Mr. Rogers, I had written:

I know the Quick contest is only in America, but I was thinking — I'm a great lover of ponies and horses. So couldn't I enter the contest? If I could I would name the pony: Goldy, Sunburst or Gift of Gold, which I like best of all.

> *Yours truly,*
> *Marsha Boulton,*
> *a Canadian pardner.*

Of course, I couldn't blame my mother for not sending the letter. And I could only blame myself for my lack of imagination. The letter wouldn't have gone to Roy anyway. Some contest droid in Milwaukee or Des Moines would have chucked it in the garbage along with all of the other Canadian posts.

But seeing the letter, with one silver horseshoe-shaped button still carefully glued to the corner, brought back all my wonderful memories of those rocking horse days of childhood when the Old West-That-Never-Was came into my living room and the guy with the best horse and the whitest hat always won the day.

There was always a happy ending. Then, the for-ever young Roy Rogers would smile that squinty-eyed smile of his and say something like "May the Good Lord take a likin' to you."

And he and Dale and Buttermilk and Trigger would ride off into the sunset.

Happy Trails, Roy. 'Til we meet again.

SOMETHING IN THE AIR

March can come in like a lion or not, as it pleases, but one thing I can be certain of — on my farm March will go out with me smelling like a lamb.

When the barn is full of sheep who are either giving birth or tending newborns, there just doesn't seem to be any way to avoid contaminating whatever environment I inhabit with some barnyard scent. It might be something as minor as a barn mitt left in the truck, or a barn sock in the laundry hamper, but there is always something sheepish lingering in the air, no matter how hard I try.

I know that I am not the only farmer effused with the scent of the workplace. Many times I have picked up the whiff of a barn in the aisles of rural supermarkets. We who spend time in barns always seem to think that we can just run in quickly, grab what we need and leave before anyone notices.

One winter, I rode all the way to the "Big Smoke" in a bus that reeked of chicken manure. The offender was a clean-cut fellow whose only mistake was wearing his distinctly well-worn barn boots in a public conveyance. No one on the bus said a word. We just wrapped ourselves tightly in our coats and opened all the windows. Stoic or stupid, you be the judge.

People who have lived on farms or know farmers learn to accept occasional olfactory pungency. Males of the species are particularly prone to not even noticing. Wives, mothers, and lovers of farmers, all have the same mantra: "You can't wear that, it's been in the barn." But sometimes, it just can't be helped.

So, I thought it would be pardonable for me take an emergency run into the Co-op farm supply store during a break in March lambing. In and out, nobody gets hurt.

Of course, I ran into Mrs. Hayward at the door. She is as legitimate a farm woman as I have ever met. In fact, she sold me my first sheep. The Hayward children were off to university and she was dispersing her flock. I didn't have a clue what I was looking for, but Mrs. Hayward helped me sort the ewes and find some "good uns." She never patronized me and she has always been there when I needed advice.

"Still got the sheep?" she asked, as we entered the store. It is the same question she asks every time we meet, and the most pleased of smiles crosses her face when I tell her that I do.

Not that I had to say a word on this particular day. I was wearing my full barn suit, and the strip of lipstick I had swiped across my mouth in the parking lot was no camouflage at all. I stank of the lambing shed. Even worse, I reeked of iodine, which was why I was at the Co-op in the first place.

When we hooked up again at the cash register, I felt compelled to explain.

"Lambing time," I said, and her big smile radiated over me like the winter sun. Lambing season had always been Mrs. Hayward's favourite.

"Big ewe butted me sideways when I was trying to clean the lamb's navel. So I expect I smell like a sheep and more," I explained, plunking a fresh bottle of iodine beside the cash register.

Mrs. Hayward nodded, seeing the iron-red iodine stain across the snowsuit and no doubt inhaling enough of its fumes to purify her sinuses for several months.

"Don't let it bother you," she said. "Father Hayward's in the calving barn so I've been taking care of the pigs for a month. Can't smell anything but pigs these days."

My senses had been so self-centred that I had failed to even notice what was definitely a piggery stench.

"You can't let farming get in the way of living," Mrs. Hayward said, in the common-sense way that she says all things. She was at the Co-op picking up some sort of pig tonic for pregnant sows.

I guess I looked fairly beaten, between the iodine, the bruise blossoming on my thigh from the ewe's butt, and the endless rounds at all hours of the day and night in the lambing barn.

Spring

"Nobody who really works on a farm looks like they just came from the beauty parlour," Mrs. Hayward offered.

I tried to remember the last time I had been to a beauty parlour and I must have looked more dejected than when we started talking. So Mrs. Hayward decided to tell me her "most mucked-up experience of all time."

Years earlier, she had been caught out in the barn late on the afternoon that one of her daughters was bringing home a likely prospect for matrimony. And not a farm boy to boot, rather an urban sort of the likeable, open-minded variety.

The whole Hayward family was assembling for supper, anticipating an announcement. Mrs. Hayward had done her usual best, planning and preparing a superb meal, including her famous homemade bread which is made from grains that are grown and ground on the farm.

At the mere mention of Mrs. Hayward's bread I became a salivating mess covered in iodine.

But that was not the end of the story.

Instead of abandoning her chores and joyfully greeting the daughter and meeting her beau, Mrs. Hayward decided she could not leave the barn before penning a loose cow with a young calf. An easy enough thing to do, she thought.

"I was just scooting them in when a darned sea gull flew through the barn and scared the cow," she explained. Sea gulls in the barn was one I hadn't heard before, but in the autumn, when the crops are being harvested, flocks of the avid scavengers accumulate in the fields. This one had apparently become disoriented.

The protective cow was so flustered that she charged the gate just as Mrs. Hayward was closing it. The latch shut, but the force of the cow sent Mrs. Hayward flying across the alley into the manure gully.

"I went sliding through all that muck for I don't know how far before I stopped," she said, holding her face and brushing her hands over her chest in remembrance.

Covered in dung, Mrs. Hayward slunk to the house and entered the basement through the cold-cellar door leading to the laundry room. She tore off her sodden barn clothes, scrubbing her face and other exposed bits in the laundry tub. Then, clad only in a yellow bath towel she retrieved from the clothes dryer, Mrs. Hayward quietly snuck up the basement stairs.

Father Hayward and the boys had returned from the fields. She could hear them laughing in the porch mud room. It was only a matter of time before her daughter began the introductions, giving Mrs. Hayward just the chance she needed to tiptoe across the kitchen and up the staircase to the comfort of a warm shower and fresh clothes.

She was halfway there, when she tripped on the cat.

"The towel was the first thing to go," she said shaking her head. "Everyone ran into the kitchen and there I was, hanging onto the counter, stark naked. My daughter was handing me the towel when I saw the diamond on her finger.

"What could I do? I stuck out my hand and welcomed the poor boy to the family. You can imagine what he said in the speech to the bride," Mrs. Hayward snorted, slapping the air with her hands.

There we were — two women stinking to high heaven, doubled over giggling in a public place in the middle of the day without an apparent care in the world.

"Can I ring this up now?" said the clerk, and we both straightened into a straighter mode.

I drove back to the farm with the truck windows open, imagining the fumes trailing after me in a purple cloud. Mrs. Hayward probably did the same thing. Neither of us would have missed our trip to town for something so insignificant as worry about the smell of our workplace.

WONDER WOMAN IN WELLINGTON BOOTS

On a farm, you live closely with the tune and the turn of the seasons. Every spring is a reminder of springs past, but every year, when the first lavender lilac bursts from bud to flower, there is a refreshing newness to celebrate.

Spring is in the air these days. I know because the neighbouring pig farmer has been keeping his barn door open and every now and then I catch a powerful whiff.

With the bedroom window just slightly open, I awake to the sounds of the barnyard — the duelling of Banty rooster crows, and the ewes calling me to feed them while their restless lambs jiggle and jump at the gate, hoping for a romp in the field.

I was feeling quite in tune with the sensuality of the farm on a recent spring morning. The flock had been fed and I let them out to play in the sunshine. There's nothing quite like the happy chaos of lambs ripsnorting around the pasture, hellbent on nothing in particular, startled by their own shadows and flabbergasted by the sight of a groundhog scurrying for cover.

In the midst of this bucolic splendour, I decided to stroll to the hay shed to fetch a few bales of fine second-cut hay for the lambs. I pushed my blue wheelbarrow, and the old black barn cat, Webster, tagged along.

I could have driven the truck, but a walk with a purpose, that was what suited my mood.

The sheep must have been watching me because I heard them coming from a distance. Two bales were on the wheelbarrow and each member of the flock was determined to be the first to have a go at finding the best leafy bits. I was standing on a platform that is raised off the ground about four feet.

In that instant, for some inexplicable reason, I decided to defend the hay.

Hollering something pertinent, like "G'it, you bad sheep," I jumped off the platform.

In that midair moment, with my straw hat slipping sideways and the cat scurrying for cover, I thought to myself, "Just think girl, you've been doing this since you were 25."

I felt like Wonder Woman in Wellington boots.

Then I landed and heard a terrible crunch.

In that sickening moment, the blue sky opened up to me and, although I saw no clouds, I knew something painful was coming my way.

It seems my once-25-year-old bones, were no longer made for flights of fancy.

Lying beside the wheelbarrow, I waved my hat at the sheep and they stopped in their tracks. It hurt, as

Spring

I knew it would, red pain in the right ankle. A few timorous lambs came forward to sniff me.

Suddenly alert, Wally, the non-sheep-herding bull terrier shot through the flock and bounded to my side, scattering lambs and licking my face with his doggy tongue, until I let out an anguished howl.

You lie there on the ground, feeling like a fool, and an old fool at that.

Of course, things must be done. Ice packs and x-rays, and "Sorry, I can't go horseback riding this Thursday."

But there's time for that, and time for stillness, especially when your left hand is planted in something that feels suspiciously like a well-aged mound of horse manure.

I spent the next ten days hobbling around with a tensor bandage supporting my swollen ankle. The good thing was that it was just a sprain. The bad thing was having to explain how it happened.

What I discovered is that the image of unstoppable youth stays with us despite the mirror's tale.

All I had to do was say, "I thought I was 25 and I jumped," and knowing looks spread across faces.

Stories flowed about childhoods spent swinging on ropes over haymows and leaping into rivers from railway trestles. They were all lithe memories from a time before knees knew how to creak. And everyone I talked to had tried in some way to recover the feeling later in life and found themselves foiled.

One poor man who had spent his youth climbing up the side of silos, told me he thought it would be a no-brainer when he decided to scale his three-storey television tower in an effort to correct a wayward antenna.

He was grappling with the mysteries of which way the wind blows channel 13 when he fell. Long before the body cast was removed, he decided to excise temptation by installing a satellite dish.

Then there was the story of someone's grandmother who insisted on picking pears well into her eighties.

Fuelled by her beverage of choice, granny mounted a stepladder and proceeded to go — quite literally — out on a limb.

She fell on a well-padded grandson who took the blame, although for the life of him he still can't figure out why. After that, grandma used her cane to whack pears out of the tree.

And a mature farm woman, whose sensible and practical wisdom I have often heeded, told me her own giddy tale about confronting a full-grown bull who was foraging in her garden.

"I don't know what I was thinking," she said. "I was just so mad. I picked up a pail and threw it at the darn bull."

In her day, she had been a passable basketball centre. She still remembers watching the arc of the pail before it slam-dunked the bull's backside.

"Best shot I ever made," she crowed. Fortunately, the startled bull charged the clothesline instead of her.

And it struck me how lucky we are to have the faultless memory of fearless youth, but how much wiser we would be to remember it rather than try to relive it.

I will remember that the next time I decide to jump anywhere on impulse. But I don't intend to become a worrywart.

I will continue to climb my metal paddock gate instead of unlocking it and going through the easy way.

I like the feeling of swinging my leg over the top of the gate.

When that gate was hung twenty years ago, it was the crowning glory that finished the job of fencing the sheep pasture. The scent of lilacs was in the air that day, too.

In the future, I guess I will have to storm the gate one rung at a time. But every time I manage to swing my leg over, I'll be saying to myself, "Just think, girl, you've been doing this since you were 25."

WALLY COMES HOME
TO ROOST

Moose and I had been talking about getting another dog as a companion to the aging yet elegant Shar-Pei, Diva, who had lost her friend the Bull-mastiff, Mingus, in an accident involving a cement truck. Moose had been devastated by that loss and swore that he would never raise another dog unless he knew it was "indestructible."

Then, I had the dream. In it, I saw Moose walking down the lane way with a miniature rhinoceros on a leash. I saw him throwing a soccer ball to the leather-plated, miniature rhinoceros and watched the little horned thing leap into the air to butt it. The wee rhino wagged its tail happily and Moose caressed its stumpy horn. It was a thoroughly satisfying dream.

A few days later, I was cajoled into watching *Hockey Night in Canada*, even though frost had not yet even threatened the garden. At some point in the broadcast, legendary curmudgeon broadcaster Don Cherry was shown cavorting with his dog Blue, a white English Bull Terrier. I was transfixed, watching the sturdy knee-high dog leaping in the air and demonstrating all sorts of manly affection to his master. I held the image of the dog's head — its huge Roman nose, those varmint-like triangular eyes, a body made out of solid muscle — and over that I superimposed a horn. Bingo! Found: a mini rhino in canine form.

Two weeks later, we were in the home of a breeder looking at a pen filled with four-week-old puppies.

There were five in the litter. Three white females with a variety of trimmings such as stripes of red on their ears and black patches on one eye. But I knew that farm life dictated that a white dog would be a high-maintenance item. One male puppy was a soft shade of chocolate brown mixed with white. And then there was a chunk of a pup with four white feet, a blaze on his face and a brindle coat, shades of brown, striped with orange — a baby rhino-tiger.

He was about the size of a beanie baby and just as floppy. When he leapt to the side of the pen in response to Moose's beckoning finger and fell backward in a perfect reverse somersault, that pup became "the one."

We passed the breeder's interview, a question-and-answer period that is akin to facing a parole board hearing. We promised to love, honour and teach the dog to obey. We learned that this life form, whose eyes were barely open, came from a long line of carefully bred champions. His pure white, milk-filled mother eyed us suspiciously, while his brindle father trotted handsomely in his outdoor run. Pictures of his grandparents and pedigrees of his great-grandparents elevated the puppy in the pen to a form of doggy royalty.

We pledged fences, the finest food and quality time. Then we wrote a big cheque. Moose muttered something about having to give the dog a car on his sixteenth birthday.

Reluctantly, we left the puppy with his litter mates for a few more weeks. At home we prepared a house for him, collected a stack of newspapers for eventualities and pondered the virtues of several puppy schools. Mostly, we debated the subject of names.

In the popular culture, Bull Terriers have had names like Spuds (the Budweiser beer dog) and Bodger (the aged hero of Sheila Burney's lost-doggy saga *The Longest Journey*.)

American Army General George Patton had a white Bull Terrier named Willie, who travelled with his master throughout World War II. There was even a legendary Bull Terrier named Patsy-Ann, who greeted ships at Juno in Alaska for many years.

Moose and I were like new parents, arguing the merits of every name from Anvil to Zydeco.

I finally retreated and decided to take my thoughts somewhere distinctly void of anything to do with puppies. I turned to poetry, grabbing from the shelves *The*

Collected Poems of Wallace Stevens. On page nine, in a poem called "The Snow Man," I found the place my thoughts needed to be.

Stevens wrote:

> *One must have a mind of winter*
> *To regard the frost and the boughs*
> *Of the pine-trees crusted with snow*

When I reminded the Moose of those lines from his favourite poet, the deed was done. I called the breeder and told her that the puppy would be named "Wallace Stevens."

On his "dog home," as we called the plastic and metal box otherwise known variously as a "cage" or a "crate," we inscribed the word "Wally."

What a difference two weeks make in one so young.

Little Wally had almost doubled in size. We swooped the pooch into a blue blanket and cuddled him all the way to the car. From the back seat, Diva the Divine observed the squirm-some thing with the waggly tail and promptly went to sleep.

At the farm, Wally sat on the front lawn trying to comprehend what had just happened to him. Diva made it patently clear that she was neither his mother nor an udder.

A huge white rooster, Foghorn Leghorn, had the run of the farm. When he saw the small brown and white "thing" on the grass, the bird ran toward "it," sending Wally into a jumping, leaping, yelping spin toward the safety of the front porch, where I was watching from a big wicker chair.

We went out together to meet the creature. I lay down on the grass, leading Wally to smother me with licks until he climbed my back and began tearing at my T-shirt. Foghorn approached and I looked up at him from the vantage of a puppy.

The old bird's feet looked like something George Lucas devised for a *Star Wars* epic. Three huge, gnarled toes with spiked toenails were topped by scaled, leathery yellow skin leading to a ball-bearing knee joint.

The rooster's eyes were black, his pupils dilated within an amber orb. Flanges of blood red flesh dribbled beneath a bone-hard beak that arched like a sickle underneath a crowning comb as jagged as the back of a stegosaur.

Then the feathers around Foghorn's neck puffed out at the sides as he drew his head back, thrusting his chest forward and raising his wings like an evil angel. Foghorn closed his eyes for an instant, and I realized that Wally had inveigled himself underneath my chin for protection from the fearsome warrior before him. The scissored beak opened, the neck drew back and the crow that emerged was so ear-splitting that I imagined it cracking the well-built clouds above his ghastly visage.

Wally shot out from under my arms. He raced around a cedar tree and tore a path through a ribbon of pansies. He stopped. Then he bolted again, hopping over my ankles, around and under my chin before I could even move. After spinning circles through my herb garden, a slightly oregano-scented handful of puppy flopped at Foghorn Leghorn's feet, gazing at the rooster as though it was some sort of icon.

Moose was standing at the kitchen door, taking in the scene. I started laughing, but he warned me against it.

"You must not laugh at Wally, you must laugh with him," he said in all seriousness.

Wally stirred, leaning far back into his haunches and mustered a mighty "yip." We laughed and Foghorn turned on the gnarly excuse that passes for a rooster's heel.

Before we introduced the puppy to his new home, Wally and Moose took a stroll down the lane. It was like watching a dream grow younger, a big man walking his future mini rhino. Indestructible.

Summer

BUTTERFLIES ARE FREE

When Bruce bought the farm, he also bought all the bells and whistles, including a perfect little gentleman-farmer's tractor in shiny red with yellow-rimmed tires. Then he dressed the tractor up with every possible accessory — a tiny perfect plough, a tiny perfect harrow, a scaled-down seeder and a cute-as-a-button pull cart. Most of the time, however, Bruce just used his tractor as a large-scale lawn mower to trim the grounds surrounding his magnificent farmhouse.

He wasn't really farming, after all. A successful businessman, Bruce described the farm variously as "a good investment" or "a place where I can get away from it all," depending on whom he was talking to. But if you were to really pin Bruce down, the truth was that he always wanted to drive a tractor. Both of his wives had run off and left him for other men, but the bond between a man and his tractor was forever.

Bruce rented his farmland to his neighbours, except for a four-acre plot along the edge of his long lane way, which he mowed relentlessly every weekend.

He was cruising along on his tractor quite happily one spring day when it struck him that he really should put his fine accessories to work. Wife Number One would have told him they were taking up valuable space. Wife Number Two would have called them silly.

So he decided he would plough half of the laneway strip and prepare it for planting, just like a real farmer.

When he finished, Bruce was quite pleased with himself, although he noticed the plough had missed a few bits. Wives Numbers One and Two would have agreed he "screwed up, as usual."

Out of respect for the land, Bruce called up a neighbour who had a large tractor and plough and hired him to "take another pass" over the field.

During the week, looking dreamily out of his floor-to-ceiling office windows at the surreal city scape, Bruce contemplated the enterprise. *What would he plant?*

He considered everything from pumpkins to garlic, but all of it seemed like too much off-tractor work to maintain himself.

So he settled on wild flowers.

A gardening magazine called a plot of wild flowers "a butterfly meadow."

Wife Number One had been allergic to pollen and Wife Number Two hated bugs of any sort. Perfect! Bruce imagined himself riding his tractor through a cloud of winged creatures, past a field dotted with daisies and black-eyed susans and wild things no one even knew the name of.

He tried to hold that vision firmly in mind when Fred at the seed store told him that the bill for two acres' worth of wild flower seed came to $690.56. Bruce knew all too well what Wives One and Two would have said to that.

Although he always tried to get out of the city early on Fridays, on this particular Friday he did not quite make it.

Halfway there, he knew he would never make it to the seed store before closing time. He pulled off the road, pulled out his cellular phone and called Fred. He quickly explained that he wanted to start seeding first thing in the morning. Fred agreed to leave the seed on the back dock of the adjoining feed mill, with a tarpaulin over it in case it rained.

Bruce picked up the seed that evening around 10 p.m. It was the first "farm related outing" he had ever taken in the new pickup truck he bought to go with the tractor. A few clouds had gathered, but there hadn't been any rain. Bruce just hoped he wouldn't have to make two trips.

At what he assumed was the designated drop-off spot, Bruce was briefly confused. A single spotlight cast an otherworldly glow on the grain mill's deserted dock. Beside half a dozen large bags of grain marked "MARTIN," a small burlap sack lay under the blue tarp. It wasn't even half full, but Bruce's name was scrawled on the bag, just as the Martin name was scrawled in black felt pen on the bulging feed bags.

"Fred must have really thought it was going to rain hard," Bruce reasoned. "I guess he didn't want to take any chances with all that expensive seed. At least," he said to himself reassuringly, "I've got enough to get started first thing."

At dawn on Saturday morning, Bruce ate a hearty breakfast. Then he grabbed the seed sack and a rake and set off to get a jump-start on his planting.

The ground had been perfectly prepared, no bumps of dirt jutting out as he had left it. Not even any tufts of grass. Bruce reached in the bag and took out a handful of seeds. Some were round, some were flat, and some just looked like specks in his hand. Then he threw the seeds away from his body and ran the rake over their landing place until all he could see on the surface was dirt.

It was fun. So Bruce did it again and again, all the while thinking that this must have been the same method of planting the first farmers had employed.

When his heritage moment ended, Bruce had succeeded in planting a strip of wildflower seeds about ten feet wide across the top of the two-acre strip.

In preparation for the long day ahead, Bruce hitched the mini-seeder to the back of the tractor and pulled the rig into the yard so that he could pour the bags of wildflower seed directly from the tailgate of the truck into the seeder. Then he drove off to the seed store to pick up the bulk of his order.

Fred greeted him at the counter and presented the bill. Bruce filled out a cheque, furtively glancing now and again out at the dock, looking for a stack of burlap sacks with his name on them.

"You think I can make it in one trip?" he asked Fred.

"I figure you already did," said Fred, tucking the cheque into his cash box.

"We usually sell it by the ounce," Fred offered, with a shake of his head. "Don't know exactly how you'd seed two acres. Some of them wildflower seeds are so bitty they just look like flecks of dust to me."

Bells and whistles started going off in Bruce's brain. He looked at his invoice, now dutifully marked "PAID IN FULL."

The $690.56 Bruce had paid was for 13 pounds of wildflower seeds at $3.32 an ounce.

While he was at the seed store, Bruce also bought enough lawn seed to cover two acres, give or take a ten-foot strip across the top.

All summer long, very expensively fed butterflies fluttered amid the blossoms of the wild flowers.

On his shiny red tractor, Bruce mowed the grass around them.

He did not speak to anyone about the profusion of wild flowers, although his neighbours did remark on how well the new lawn seed had taken.

And, for the first time in his life, Bruce was happy that his wives had run off with other men.

You don't have to explain anything to your neighbours, or your tractor.

THE BAT WHISPERER

You don't hear them twittering like birds and you don't see them fluttering like silent butterflies. Instead, bats tend to surprise you.

One evening you might leave a neighbour's house after dark and look up at the moon, and see them zipping across its luminous face like little clouds of teacup-sized asteroids.

You might be out standing on a cottage dock watching the stars, when all of a sudden some small, dark, winged thing whips past you.

Or you might be in the parlour of an old farmhouse when one sneaks its way in and starts zooming around looking for a way out.

Bats generally keep their distance, but they do show up at the oddest of times in the oddest of places. And, even though I like bats, they always leave me with an eerie feeling and goose bumps as though I have been the subject of a visitation.

My first bat in the parlour was a comedy of errors that I am sure has been repeated in countless households.

Summer

We had not yet "settled" on the farm and the furnishings were as scant as a university student's first apartment. In fact, we joked about the ancient, round, wooden hydro spool that we used as a coffee table for the first year.

The kitchen, the family room and the bedrooms were equipped, but the parlour was so vacant that we installed a ping-pong table for rainy weekend recreation.

The bat appeared during a particularly rousing, four-handed game. I had successfully pinged the ball over the net and Moose raised his racket to pong it back when his partner, Mike, took a heck of a whack at something in midair. My partner, Janet, let her paddle drop to the floor and commenced jogging in place with her lips pursed, all the while emitting a back-of-the-throat hysterical hum.

Moose was under the table looking for the ping-pong ball, while Mike held his racket over his eyes and squinted into the distant corners of the room.

I was preparing to utter a statement akin to "Pray, what was that?" when the thing made another pass over the table. Between Janet's humming and Moose's sub-tabular fumbling for the ping-pong ball, it was hard to detect any sound associated with the assault. It was like a zipper opening in midair. Then it was gone.

Mike, an advertising executive who had been to summer camp as a child, immediately identified the creature as a bat. Those of us familiar with *Dracula* (the movie) immediately dove for cover. Three of us were still cowering under the table when Mike walked into the room with a kitchen broom which he planned to use to flush the bat out.

No sooner had Mike waved his corn-husk wand than the bat exited the parlour, looped through the kitchen and headed for the family room.

In the space of a short eternity, we learned everything Mike knew about bats. They are not evil, blood-sucking things, unless you happen to be in some disappearing South American jungle, where the spread of rabies and other blood-borne diseases was once, allegedly, a cause of concern with so-called "vampire bats."

They eat millions and millions and millions of mosquitoes, so in my book bats are a very good thing.

Hundreds of them can live in a small space, where they sleep during the day, hanging upside down, enclosed in the leathery membrane that creates wings between their long spidery fingers.

They are the only mammal that flies.

Most important, they don't bump into things because they bounce a high-pitched sound frequency off objects and they can judge by the echo how close it is, in a bizarre sort of rodent radar. But this very unique built-in radar makes confined air-borne bat behaviour a little bizarre and erratic.

As a teenager, Mike explained in a quiet almost reverent tone, he had done a whole summer camp project on bats, but he had never actually seen one in the flesh.

Equipped with flashlights, binoculars and a trout fishing net, we repaired to the family room to capture the bat.

Janet tentatively, reluctantly, looked behind the sofa.

Nothing.

I swatted cushions with the broom.

The men illuminated the dark corners of the four-teen-foot ceiling with a flashlight, discovering a variety of bat-like cobwebs.

Janet was bravely lifting the hydro spool, when Mike shouted, "Got 'em."

We followed his finger to the gaping mouth of the stuffed, twenty-pound salmon which was the first *objet d'art* to hang in the farmhouse. There was a brownish blob about the size of two walnuts clinging like a leech on the inside jaw.

This was no time for brooms.

Janet was again jogging in place, trying not to hum and give away her location. Both men wrestled for the fishnet, until it was mutually agreed that Moose, being the taller and the more experienced fisherman, would try to "capture" the now motion-less bat.

He did manage to loop the fishnet over the salmon's mouth, but then the bat moved. Moose jumped back and the fish fell head first into the net which could only contain one-third of its hand-painted corpse.

In the meantime, the bat zipped out through a hole in the net and flew directly at Janet, who instinctively raised the ping-pong paddle to which she still furtively clung, like some anti-bat talisman. It was a futile gesture. The bat simply zipped around it.

The light in the room was not the brightest, but we all caught shadowy glimpses of the bat as it flew erratically around our heads.

Sharp-eyed Mike spotted it leaving the room through an open window, and we all gathered to look for it but, alas, it was gone and our game of ping-pong had somehow lost its lustre.

Years later, bats became a trendy eco-species. Environmentally friendly nature stores and catalogues became purveyors of bat houses.

Laws were passed in certain states against the arbitrary poisoning of bats.

Even though the parishioners might have had other thoughts, bat rights were entrenched in many a New England church belfry.

But the blood-sucking, rabies-invested bat mystique lingers on.

I was quietly fingering through the ladies' athletic socks at my local Stedman's store when a curdled cry rang out from the back storage room. A shaken teenaged clerk emerged wringing her hands, close to tears.

A "thing" had flown at her from behind a box on the top shelf where the Christmas tree lights had been stashed six months earlier.

It was no bird, she knew that much.

It had a face; beady eyes, flat-sort of nose, pointy little ears and a mouth, maybe even teeth. She was describing a teacup-sized flying animal that looked like a cross between a monkey and a Chihuahua, so I knew it had to be a bat.

The assistant store manager, a mature woman with years of retail experience, called the store owner for advice. No answer. Then she called the Town office to get them to send over the animal control officer. Alas, the animal control officer in the town of Mt. Forest does not "do" bats.

The next step was closing up the store and calling in the cops. Two young mothers had already given up on buying diapers and fled to the safety of the street. The only shopper left in the store was a light-fingered youth, who sucked in his breath so hard when the clerk described the beast, that the CD he had tucked in his pants fell right to the base of his pant-leg.

If it had been a skunk, I might have thought twice, but, having had previous bat invasion experience, I figured I could give it a go.

Deborah, the shaken teenaged clerk, pointed me toward a pile of fallen cardboard boxes where she had seen the thing headed.

Sure enough, under a wad of tissue paper at the bottom of the third smallish box that I examined, there was a small brown blob lying with its back to me.

I went back into the store and found one of those splatter-screen kitchen utensils you use to keep frying oil at bay with, and fixed it over the top of the bat box.

By this time the assistant store manager had managed to get her brother-in-law on the phone. He was a Town Councillor and vowed to send over a road maintenance crew who were on their lunch break to straighten things out. No doubt his next call had been to the local newspaper, with the potential headline "Councillor Rids Town Store of Bat" looming large in next Wednesday's town weekly, *The Confederate.*

Stedman's back door opens out onto the local tavern parking lot. I eased the box outside and turned it on its side. The blob slid to the bottom. No sooner was the splatter pan removed than the bat whizzed out of the box, across the parking lot, over the dumpster, around the laundromat air vents and into the surrounding tree branches.

The road crew greeted me on their way out of the tavern. I told them the bat had escaped, so they could go back to their lunch. There were no headlines about flying mammals that week, but I did get a free pair of athletic socks and a toque for my troubles.

WALLY'S WORLD

I was told in no uncertain terms by the breeder, when first I dared inquire after a Bull Terrier puppy, that one does not "just *have* a Bull Terrier, you have a Bull Terrier *experience*."

Then, of course, there is the issue of who has who.

The story of Bill Brodsky, a long-time Bull Terrier owner, was conveyed by way of illustration.

Bill Brodsky said, "Bull Terriers? Had 'em all my life. I was twelve before I had realized he wasn't my brother."

In the beginning, I did not quite understand what Bill was getting at.

For the first three months of their lives, Bull Terriers are more piranha than puppy. Underneath that loopy nose lies a mouthful of miniature harpoon tips in search of a juncture to puncture.

It took Wally less than an hour to rip the voice box out of the fuzzy-wuzzy squeaking teddy bear that was to have been his first toy. And he would have eaten that had I not risked my digits to pry it away.

That's another thing. Bull Terriers will eat almost anything.

In Wally's first week at the farm, a number of things went missing. For instance, the rubber lamb nipple on the bottle I keep in the barn to feed milk to orphaned lambs.

Where oh where could it be, I wondered, until the mangled nipple turned up in Wally's stool.

I am still looking for a blue sock. And there is missing lingerie that I do not wish to discuss.

Nails, rocks, tree branches and car keys are just a few of the things that have been recovered from intrepid Bull Terrier guts. If they don't eat your wallet, as a consequence of these extreme gastronomic tastes, they can readily negate its reason for being.

When Wally was a puppy, he woke up one Sunday morning feeling a little bit peckish. That is to say that instead of leaving the house like a Stealth Bomber launched off the front porch, scattering all the guinea fowl into the branches of the maple tree, he just walked.

Because of its shape, the face of a Bull Terrier looks like a bicycle seat with eyes. I looked deeply into his. Normally, there is a certain look, a devil-may-care glint that now just wasn't there. All was not well in Wally's world.

He did not have a temperature. No agonized howls. Just not right. When he would not eat, I feared for his life.

I called Dr. Ron, my small-animal vet at home. Dr. Ron loves Bull Terriers. If it were not for his allergies, he would probably have as many bullies as he has children — which is quite a few. Having Wally as a client gives Dr. Ron great pleasure, but he did not like the sound of what I was telling him over the phone.

The upshot was that Moose and me and Wally ended up spending Sunday afternoon in the Emergency Ward of the University of Guelph's Veterinary Clinic.

If Wally had a blockage or an obstruction or something else too hideous to contemplate, the university, and one of the finest animal clinics in the world, would have whatever tools might be necessary to deal with it.

That day we considered ourselves very fortunate to be living only 40 minutes away from Guelph. How ironic, I thought, that I should be revisiting my alma mater, where I first learned about sheep, with a dog who some people think looks like Babe, the sheep-pig, of Hollywood fame.

When the doctor came into the examining room, Wally perked right up. Pretty women have that effect on him.

His vital signs were good. His tail started wagging again. Sprawled on his back, a trance-like ecstasy spread over his face when she palpitated his stomach. Then we faced her for the diagnosis.

"There's no question he's got into something but it's just given him an upset tummy," the good doctor said. She had perched on the examining table, cross-legged. Wally was beside her, sitting as he does, like an old Italian gentleman with legs akimbo, contemplating a bocchi ball game.

The prescription: soft food, plenty of fluids. Wally lifted his head and looked back at her adoringly. Then Moose and I noticed that he was experiencing his first erection and the glint was back in his eyes.

All the way home, Wally rolled happily in the back seat, yelping joyfully until he finally decided to rest his head on Moose's shoulder with his paws dangling behind the head rest. It looked as though Moose had grown a second head. Wally stared intently at the road ahead, as though *he* were driving the car. He remained in that position for the remainder of the trip back to the farm.

I was starting to understand what Bill Brodsky meant.

We never did find out what made Wally peckish. He ate a whole bowl of chicken soup that night and proceeded to hucklebutt the house.

Hucklebutting is a bully thing. It involves running at top speeds, making impossible U-turns around table legs and rearranging cushions. Sometimes whole furniture patterns are re-arranged. The dog resembles a snub-nosed torpedo with legs and a twisted sense of direction. It is all part of the "experience."

In keeping with the nature of his breed, Wally likes to dominate everything in his environment. That includes us.

We were told: Rules must be made and stuck to or the bully takes over as pack leader. "No" must mean "no"; be firm but friendly, and so forth.

That worked with Wally for a while, until he caught on. Once he figured out how malleable companion humans can be, how putty-like in the paws of a puppy, he seemed to instinctively understand how flexible those things called rules really are.

Yes, he sleeps on the bed.

Okay, so he also sleeps under the covers.

And when Wally gets too warm, he tunnels to the bottom of the bed, pushes the sheet open and spills onto the floor in the middle of the night with an unceremonious "thud."

Shortly thereafter, he recklessly jumps across the pillows and tunnels back in place.

Wally also snores. Loudly. And he burps and does other things that are all too human.

Then there is this thing about balls and Bull Terriers.

Anything round that has the potential to roll captivates them. The problem is that most balls cannot withstand bully play. Tennis balls split, baseballs shred, all of which can lead to a dreaded "blockage" if the remnants are swallowed.

Enthusiastic loving chomps altered the form and function of dozens of basket, volley and soccer balls.

After far too many trips to the sporting-goods store, I decided to dominate.

The rule I set sounds demanding, but the power of the orb was such that Wally quickly learned and obeyed. He can play with a ball *only* if he has something else in his mouth to act as a tooth guard. And the only tooth guard strong enough to withstand the jaws of an 80-pound Bull Terrier is a brutally tough rubber thing called a "Kong."

Wally has Kongs in various sizes and shapes. Large black Kongs are for outdoor play, red Kongs stay inside. Kongs are not allowed in the barn. And without a Kong, a ball cannot be in play. Simple.

There is nothing simple, however, about the way Wally plays with his balls. Having decided to abide by my rules, he has created a whole playbook of his own.

Wally's game of soccer involves controlling the ball with his front paws and propelling it toward its goal with his nose. Throw it and he does headers as good as anything you will ever see in World Cup play. He leaps into the air, rising twice his height and smashing the ball with his head. He is without question the Pele of the dog world.

His field of play is the front lawn of the farmhouse. His boundaries are a walkway, the lane way and the shadow of a large cedar tree. Within these self-imposed confines lies "the goal," a raised wooden flower box that runs the length of the front porch.

Human companion players should not set foot on Wally's field. They must stay in the lane way. Wally shoots the ball at them. If the human misses, he scores an automatic goal and wags heartily. Then the human must shoot the ball back, trying to propel it into the side of the flower bed goal while Wally fields and guards. As games go, I must say I quite enjoy it.

When he is not playing soccer, Wally also bounces tennis balls off his nose. And basketballs, volleyballs and even this fall, a football.

Another game is ball-in-the-pail. Wally started out rolling my hard plastic barn pails with his chest around the yard at a furious rate. This was most disconcerting, since it is the mark of a farmer that we never willingly part with any five-gallon pail. For the first time in my life on the farm, I began hanging my pails on hooks drilled into overhead barn beams.

Then Wally discovered my grain pans and such. A hard black plastic pan with low sides proved the perfect tool for Wally to scoop up his soccer balls. With the ball balanced in the pan, he proceeds to run around the property in ever-expanding figure-eights. Sometimes for hours on end.

Moose actually believes that Wally communicates with him through the ball, any ball. Bull Terriers raise anthropomorphism to a mystical level.

It is not a dog I would recommend to just anyone. Keeping up with "the experience" takes a certain energy and you have to have room on your face for a lot of laugh lines, but I have come to know exactly what Bill Brodsky was talking about.

As far as I'm concerned, one can never have too many brothers.

IN CLUMPS AND BOUNDS

The voice at the other end of the phone line sounded frazzled.

"I need clumps. You have lots of them, don't you?" asked Lela, an old friend from the days when I was acquainted with socialites and the whims of those who entertain in a grand style.

The "clumps" in question were large masses of flowers. It was the early 1990s and gardening had suddenly become ultra-fashionable among the ladies-who-previously-lunched. Lela was hostessing a back-yard fund-raiser, and the pedestrian planting of pansies and geraniums she had at poolside just would not cut the mustard. Instead, Lela wanted to have massive displays of peonies and poppies, lupins and lilies.

"A sort of flagrant Olde English garden," was how she put it.

Well, my flower beds at the farm do tend to have a "clumpy" look, I suppose. But as I explained to Lela, it is simply not possible to dig up "clumps" in full bloom and expect them to survive a two-hour drive to new digs without having them suffer collateral wilting.

"Clumps," I told her, are the consequence of allowing a plant to put down roots, grow strong and spread. A decent clump can take a few years of nurture. Then you divide the clump and create some more.

A finely clumped garden can take years to develop. But to the gardener, there's a story behind each clump, and every gardener surely knows which clump is the mother clump and which ones are the siblings.

For instance, I can trace all of my clumps of bushy bleeding hearts to one bush planted at the side of the farmhouse. Her progeny are everywhere. Some live in my mother's garden, one lives in Toronto and the other lives beside a neighbour's mailbox. The mother of all clumps is often the pride of the garden.

Lela ended up going to her local upscale nursery and commissioning large clay pots, overstuffed with annual blooms that managed to approximate the image of flagrant something-or-others. She was happy.

As the millennium rushes to an end at the speed of data through fibre-optic cable, the concept of "instant gardening" seems to have taken a stranglehold on urbanites, a phenomenon which is both amusing and disturbing.

For the price of enough seeds to populate a garden for a century, consumers are invited to subscribe to glossy magazines that promises to tell them how to spend their way into an "instant" garden.

Books, television programs, whole satellite television networks are devoted to making the solitary and contemplative pursuit of a private haven into a burden-free hobby that takes about as much time and effort as flipping a burger on the barbecue. Where's the fun in that?

It gets worse.

My friend Claire, a woman who is as urban(e) as women get, who I suspect subscribes to several glossy gardening magazines, who I know maintains a library of books about things like "You and Your Patio-Stone-Friendly Garden," has somehow managed to create her own oasis of charm and maintain a devoted interest in each and every one of her plants.

What she discovered in the affluent back alleys of her neighbourhood was a shocking disregard for life forms that do not eat pâté.

"My gawd, they dumped a dozen rhododendrons in a bin behind the new condo," wailed Claire. In broad daylight, she executed a rhododendron rescue. Four of the mature plants fit comfortably in the trunk of her Audi.

It seems the rhododendrons had flowered suitably on the rooftop garden, but their residual leafy green was no longer required. Someone decreed: "Out with the old, in with the new," and showy annuals likely replaced the uprooted rhododendrons.

Eight out of twelve rescued rhododendrons are now thriving in Claire's garden.

In fact, she has made the pursuit of homeless plants something of a hobby.

Dried fuchsia hanging baskets in need of a drink find themselves drenching at the edge of her backyard lily pond.

One whole section of her garden is devoted to "found bulbs," leftover municipal daffodil and tulip residue that would otherwise be composted into flowerless obscurity in some landfill.

Claire's garden is full of surprises, a riot of colours bound by the theme that every plant is a wanted plant, even those that are unwanted by others.

She is as proud of her urban clumps as I am of my country clumps. Our gardens have deep roots and character. That's what makes us happy — gardens, rural or urban, that grow flagrantly, in clumps and bounds.

ANTI-NOAH'S FARM

When the two reverends, Doris and Daniel, were granted a rural ministry, they thought their prayers had been answered.

They had ministered in inner cities, outlying suburbs and small towns. Wherever they were asked, they went. But in their dreams, they imagined serving a peaceful country church, the kind where every family has its own pew and the organist knows all the hymns by heart. Somewhere nearby the church, they dreamed of having their own little farm.

And so it came to pass.

The church was a fine yellow-brick building with an unimposing steeple and a gleaming oak door. Sunlight dappled through the stained-glass windows into the sanctuary, and well-worn hymnals and prayer books lined the pews.

In the lower level, the Sunday School rooms and kitchen/dining area looked out on a country road and a pasture field, where curious cows gathered on the Lord's Day to watch the comings and goings and listen to the joyful sounds.

Along with the church, the two reverends were provided with their ultimate fantasy. It was a small house by most standards, but the front porch looked out over a pond draped with willow trees.

On warm summer afternoons, the reverends would sit in their rocking chairs, counting the turtles sunbathing on a log and listening for the *plop* of bull-frogs. At dusk, the deer would come to drink.

Behind the plain frame house, there was a small red barn with three horse-sized stalls and a couple of open pens. The mow could hold about a hundred bales of hay and still leave the pigeons with fluttering space.

There was a fenced paddock and a small pasture facing onto a maple bush that turned the colour of fireside flame in autumn. Between the house and the barn, a path was lined with knee-high sunflowers called "Teddy Bears," bordering a garden plot that was twice the size of the ground floor of the house.

In all the years of their marriage and their minis-tering, this was exactly what the reverends had hoped for.

Neither of them knew much about country life or farming, but they found themselves embraced by their neighbours. Everything from firewood to fresh eggs showed up on the stoop of the veranda, with a friendly face behind it all, asking only a blessing in return.

Often, after the Sunday service, a parishioner would offer an invitation to come for tea, to help celebrate an anniversary or just to take a tour of the farm and stay for a barbecue. It was at a barbecue, when Doris mused aloud about how she had always wanted to know what it felt like to care for animals.

The Velkon family farm was a devoted dairy operation, but the children had their own "special projects." In an old driving shed, Billy Velkon and his sister, Mary, raised rabbits and an assortment of exotic chickens. When the kids took Doris on a tour, she spotted one huge grey rabbit sitting forlornly in a pen all by itself.

"That's Mambo," explained nine-year-old Mary, solemnly. "She can't have babies anymore, so we have to get rid of her."

Doris furled her brow into a question mark. Billy, who was a few years older than Mary, whispered in the reverend's ear.

"Dad's gonna shoot her. It won't hurt or anything."

Doris reached into the pen and stroked the old rabbit's fur. Mambo raised her twitchy nose, revealing clear blue eyes circled with pink.

"You could have her if you want. We have lots of extra pens, too," said Mary. "She never bites."

Doris did not hesitate. She knew Daniel would agree that it would be a sin to leave a creature awaiting certain death for the sole crime of infertility, especially when they had a whole empty barn at their disposal.

The two reverends left the Velkon farm with Mambo in the back seat.

One barren bunny was just the beginning.

At church the following week, Reverend Daniel delivered a sermon titled "A Second Chance for All God's Creatures."

He trod a delicate furrow in farm country, where the dead-stock trucks routinely pick up any half-dead "downer" cows, and the last thing some crippled piglets see is the head of a shovel.

Later that Sunday, the widow Rachel Hunter stopped by, ostensibly to drop off a peach pie for Doris.

"I enjoyed the sermon," she told Daniel. "It reminded me of how my late husband Bill kept an old blind boar in the back of the piggery for years after he served any useful purpose. Huge old boar, he was, but a gentle soul. Used to come when Bill called to him."

Then she paused, lost in memory, and rocked her chair.

"Suii, Suii, Here come, Chop, here come," whistled Rachel, recalling the sing-song call Bill had used to summon the blind pig. Then she sighed. "Bill died a year to the day after he buried Chop. He always said he wouldn't go before that pig."

In the week following the sermon, the two reverends heard many such stories — about old faithful ploughing horses, dried-up milk cows, three-legged barn cats and even a flightless barn pigeon. They were all long-gone animals, remembered from a time before "the bottom line" was a serious threat to every farm, a time when love and loyalty were weighed along with Total Daily Nutrient Consumed and Estimated Value of Production.

Before long, the reverends ended up opening their barn to a few more strays. From the outset, Daniel and Doris made one simple rule: since they were not in the business of farming, they would not be in the business of breeding animals. They would take one of any creature, and do their best to find homes for the rest.

That was the beginning of the Anti-Noah's Farm.

The animals came in one by one. There was Pouch, a miniature donkey who had arthritis. Doris simply could not resist the mouse-grey, long-eared creature. The fact that he enjoyed having his back massaged made Pouch even more endearing. Of an afternoon, Doris would look out her kitchen window and see the donkey sitting contentedly on his rump, like a large dog. It always made her smile.

Then a really large dog came to join Pouch in his reveries.

Tiny's owners were almost frantic when Reverend Daniel answered their advertisement in the weekend edition of the city newspaper that the church organist passed along to him each Sunday. They were computer specialists who had been transferred to assignments in Asia. Tiny was their Great

Dane, a six-year-old spayed female who could knock Mambo the rabbit off her feet with one giant lick.

The only creature that Tiny did not try to lick was Iggy, an old white goose, who hissed and snapped anytime the black dog's shadow crossed his own.

In a cage beside Mambo, a male guinea pig and a long-haired female hamster snuffled around in a bed of shavings that was cleaned twice a week by eleven-year-old Kelly Lambert, whose younger brother had severe allergies.

Kelly was also happy to tend to the needs of Melissa, a Vietnamese pot-bellied pig who once lived in town, but outgrew her circumstances and enraged her owner's neighbours by rooting in their gardens.

At the reverends', Melissa rooted around Pouch and wallowed with the turtles in the pond, where a mateless Canada Goose endlessly cruised.

A one-eyed goat named Sam and a grandmother ewe named Flossy shared a stall in the barn and a bounty of windfall apples in their pasture. If a shepherd was too busy to keep a bottle-fed lamb, Doris would take it and raise it for a while until it could go back to the flock. When she nurtured a runt calf, the weaker of a set of twins, she impressed everyone. The buttery brown Jersey named Daisy became Jennifer Talbot's 4H calf and they took first prize in the fall fair, with due credit given to "Reverend Godmother Doris."

Every once in a while, someone would drop off a kitten. Doris and Daniel found homes for them, except for Cal, a calico cat, who was the resident mouser and lap cat. Cal eyed each new addition to the farm with suspicion but, as long as they stayed off his cushion on the front porch, the kingdom remained peaceable.

Semi-regulars became regular attendees at the church and the Sunday School was packed. The reverends' kitchen was always open to anyone who just wanted to talk. People often stopped by to check on the animals and offer advice, as well as everything from feed to fencing.

News of Doris and Daniel's success in the rural community reached the church hierarchy. Doris and Daniel received a formal request for a delegation of observers to attend a service.

This made the two reverends nervous. They well knew success often spelled transfer. They broached the possibility with a few of the church elders, concerned only about what would happen to the animals if they were required to move on.

Doris delivered the sermon on the fateful Sunday. The leader of the church delegation, Reverend Ron Whipple, and half a dozen assorted observers were duly welcomed and presented with gifts, including a selection of homemade preserves.

As her theme, Doris chose "The Farm as Sanctuary," which seemed appropriate since afterward the congregation and the visitors were all invited to attend a tea at the reverends' homestead which, after all, was nothing if not a sanctuary.

Doris and Daniel did everything they could to minimize the visibility of the animals, but, on a farm, out of sight is seldom out of mind. There was nothing they could do to minimize the smells and sounds of their growing menagerie. Pouch brayed from his stall, while Sam and Flossy *baaed* anxiously and the old goose squawked.

In the kitchen and in the yard, people sipped their tea and chewed their cookies as though oblivious, while the observers twitched and arched their brows.

"I do so love to see the pig. Where's the pig?" inquired the widow Hunter. Then, realizing she had interrupted a potentially religious conversation between Reverend Daniel and Reverend Whipple, she whipped out her hand and introduced herself.

"Rachel Hunter," she said. "My late husband Bill had a blind pig named Chop." Then she wandered off, calling "Suii, Suii," under her breath.

The Sunday Schoolers broke the lid off things. They excitedly rushed the barn to see what was new and revisit what was old. Soon the paddock was full and kids were sitting on the porch, legs dangling into the petunias, petting Mambo and crew, along with a squirmy ferret named Fuzzbuster. Hammy Hamster ran up Mary Velkon's right arm, under her blouse, and down the left, dangerously close to Cal's cat cushion. There was a momentary panic.

Then Pouch sat down and brayed, distracting everyone, except for the untended pig who discovered that rooting in Doris's garden was much more rewarding than rooting around Pouch.

The Reverend Whipple and his gentrified delegation were somewhat taken aback. They frowningly sipped their tea and watched as Doris and the choir mistress chased Melissa the pig out of the garden and then plucked a few carrots for a donkey that apparently did nothing except sit on his hind end and *hee haw.*

Sam the goat tried to nibble one of the delegate's patent-leather shoes, a material that interested him greatly since he had not seen such shiny potential food on the farm.

"It's eating my foot," screamed the patent-shoed woman, who jumped back, leaving the shoe in Sam's bearded mouth. Young Kelly Lambert grabbed it away.

"Sam just wanted to nibble it," he muttered, wiping the slightly scarred shiny red pump on the thigh of his good Sunday pants and handing it back to the hobbled delegate.

Then Kelly stroked old Sam's head and the goat rubbed against him.

"Sam's only got one eye," he said to no one in particular. "He's no good for anything and he should be dead."

Reverend Whipple took a step forward to hear the boy more closely.

"Fact is, everything on this place would be dead if it weren't for the reverends," Kelly continued, shoving his hands deep in his pockets and talking to the ground.

"My brother coughed real bad because he was allergic to Hammy and Ginny, and my dad told me to say goodbye to them. They would have had their skulls crushed with the mallet, sure as anything, if the reverends didn't take them in. Not to say my dad's bad, he didn't think he had a choice. Just like Mr. Velkon would have shot Mambo soon as look at her because she was just taking up space. And old Pouch, he can't do much of anything."

Kelly's father joined him and put his arm around the boy. Don Lambert, like his son, was spare with his words.

"Kelly's right," he said. "Until the reverends came, we all tried not to think much about animals — I mean, a pet is a pet, but if it interferes with your life it's got to go, that's how I thought. Farmers can't have animals taking up space and not producing, not when feed's as dear as it is."

"Don's right," said a voice from the crowd. "The reverends raised two of my orphan lambs and now those lambs have lambs of their own."

Jennifer Talbot told her prize-winning calf story.

"Now Daisy gives so much milk that I bring some extra over for the pig every week," she said, and there was a small, spontaneous round of applause.

"The reverends are godparents to all these animals," said Jennifer, "so if you make them leave, you make all of the animals into orphans. Then everything will go back just the way it was."

People left quietly after that. Falling away in tidy knots, they seemed to melt down the lane. Alone with Reverend Whipple and two carloads of delegates, Doris and Daniel shivered under stoic skin. The yard was still.

"You've done a fine job here," began the Reverend Whipple, in a solemn tone that matched his grey eyes.

"I mean it's fantastic what you've done. Just to see those people and the connection you've made and the obvious Love the good Lord bestows, and the animals . . . "

He was clearly touched.

In the paddock, the pot-bellied pig started rooting. Her steady *unh, unh, unh* grunts forming a background rhythm section to the chorus of praise from the chattering visitors.

By the time they were done, Fuzzbuster the ferret was stuffed with pound cake and draped around the collar of one of the visiting dignitaries.

The patent-shoed observer fed the goat a carrot and quietly took Doris aside.

"I don't want to impose," she began, "but my sister is quite ill, in and out of the hospital all the time. The problem is, she still has this budgie, but she thinks the world of him."

"We've never had a budgie," says Doris. "Tell your sister we would be happy to take care of the little fellow for as long as she needs. That's what we're here for."

The two reverends were not going anywhere.

Instead, the Church sent them a brass sign to hang on their mailbox. All it says is "Sanctuary."

THE SQUIRT

Mabel was the youngest of a family of five. Her nearest sibling was six years older, and she was the only female. The boys called her "Squirt." She had always been tiny. Mabel enjoyed the privilege of being pampered and cooed over when she was a toddler, but by the age of five she began to feel left out of the pack.

Her brothers all had barn chores to do before they cleaned themselves up and headed off together for the school bus. When they came home, there were more chores. Then they all sat down for the evening meal, and it seemed to Mabel that her brothers had their own secrets and their own language.

They talked about teachers and compared notes. They told their father about a calf with a sore leg or a plan they had to build a new gate. When they went to their rooms to do their homework, Mabel would listen through the door and hear them talking about everything from hockey players to girls.

That summer, Mabel decided to become one of them. She pulled her hair back into a tight pony-tail and announced that she was ready to help with the chores. Tagging after them toward the barn, Mabel suddenly found herself scooped up in the firm arms of her father and deposited squarely back in the farmhouse kitchen.

"Barn's no place for a squirt like you," he said.

There were things that Mabel was allowed to do. Under the watchful eye of her mother, she trailed around the garden pulling weeds and picking peas. Perched on a soda pop crate, she reached into chicken nests and gathered fresh eggs. When the dog's water bowl was half full, she filled it.

Still, the brothers seemed to stream through the house and fill it with life and excitement that Mabel was missing. They would come bursting through the screen door, dusty, tanned and poking each other to be the first to get into the refrigerator. They placed bets with each other about who could load and unload a wagon fastest. Everything about them seemed larger than her own life.

As the summer drew to a close, Mabel felt more and more left out. No one seemed to care what she did, as long as she didn't do it near them.

The last job the boys had to do on the farm that summer was setting a row of fence poles along a stretch of hard gravelly ground.

The poles had to be set into the ground a good three feet and they were to be placed no more than twelve feet apart.

Once the boys had dug the holes, using a combination of the tractor and auger along with pick axes and shovels, their father said he would measure each one and, if the job was done to his satisfaction, the whole family would spend the last Saturday of the summer in the big city watching a professional baseball game.

Mabel's mother gave her a wink and told her that she would have to work with the boys to qualify. The four brothers groaned, mumbling about the "Squirt" getting in their way.

The boys had three days to dig the holes while their father was away at a cattle sale. It was dry, miserable work. Mabel helped the boys pile rocks at the edge of each hole. The rest of the time she had to stand three holes away from them when the tractor was running and the post-hole digger gyrated its way through the tough clay ground.

"Not deep enough," said Mabel sitting on the edge of one of the first holes.

"What would you know, Squirt," the boys said, almost in unison.

Then Mabel slid into the hole.

"See, half-my-head short," she said, peering up at them with her nose on a level with the lip of the post hole. "I'm just exactly three feet tall."

When Mabel's father came to inspect the fence line, he found the holes neatly dug with a post lined up next to each one.

"Looks good, but the tape will tell a truer story," the farmer said, taking out his faithful tape measure.

Mabel's oldest brother pushed her forward. She looked up at her father shyly.

"I'm the fence measurer," she said, "and the hole measurer, too."

Mabel's father gave her a quizzical look, and then the boys took over.

One grabbed the tape measure and, while Mabel stood on the tab at the end, he ran it to the top of her head.

"Squirt's exactly three feet," he said.

The two other brothers picked Mabel up and lowered her into the hole. The earth around it was perfectly level with the top of Mabel's head.

Outside the hole, Mabel crouched down and rolled four somersaults, landing her exactly at the opening of the second hole.

Again two brothers lowered her, patting the top of her head to show their father that the hole had met the measure of his daughter.

"A full Squirt" the boys called it, and Mabel gritted her teeth.

The job was pronounced well done and Mabel rode back to the farm house on her father's shoulders. Her mother was waiting on the porch with a small package wrapped in shiny paper, a present for Mabel.

It was a tape measure tucked inside a baseball cap.

"Being a Squirt only lasts so long," said Mabel's mother.

Sure enough, when Mabel was measured in her fine new cap she was a full tick taller than three feet.

No one ever called Mabel "Squirt" again.

Fall

NO RAM OF MINE

I've been thinking a lot about sex and sheep recently. This is not as unhealthy as it sounds, since the breeding season for sheep is coming up soon. As soon as there is a nip of chill in the night air, some trigger in their brains activates sheep hormones and translates into lust. The ram is the best barometer of this.

And all of that nasty business with President Clinton caused me to have even greater admiration for the ram who serves as the sire for my flock than I already did.

My ram never lies.

He never makes excuses.

And he is unabashedly polygamous. The worst thing that he could admit to a Grand Jury would be his incessant, libido-inspired penchant to jump fences.

I've known sheep sent to the wool factory for less.

Obviously sheep and other animals have simpler lives than the President. So I have resented certain American news reporters who have compared the behaviour of Mr. Clinton variously to that of a dog, a goat and, yes, even a ram.

Fall

Sheep don't have sex for fun. At least, I don't think they do.

And there is not much romance involved. Certainly no exchanging of gifts.

There is nothing furtive about what they do in virtually any aspect of their sheepish lives.

Quite simply, sheep have no shame and a ram wouldn't know how to look embarrassed if he tried.

You would never find a ram looking apologetic about having had sex with a young ewe.

And since the whole flock is his harem, there is no First Ewe to answer to.

It is perfectly natural for a ram to have sex in his workplace, since sex is his one and only job in life.

Mind you, I don't think a ram could pull off serving as the leader of the most powerful nation in the free world — but I do resent the American media comparing the behaviour of their wayward President to that of an innocent male sheep.

I've kept a dozen or so rams on the farm over the years. My first was a feisty fellow called Cronkite, because I wanted him to be as trustworthy and steady on the plough as his newsman namesake. Then I had my *Star Wars* sire, Jedi, followed by the outlaw brothers, Waylon and Willie.

From Rambo to Lord Randall, none of my rams would give the time of day to the likes of Monica Lewinsky, even if she was to be wearing a blue wool dress.

All of the tawdry, mawkish, demeaning news that has emerged about what goes on behind closed Oval Office doors has nothing to do with the morality of sheep. Sheep have no morality, which seems to be the only thing that Bill Clinton and my present ram, Cisco the Kid Maker, have in common.

I was watching the flock one evening last week. Some people might think that watching sheep is about as interesting as staring at wallpaper, but it is a very important aspect of shepherding.

There is almost as much reading between-the-lines to do with watching sheep as there was in having to translate an American President's version of certain events.

It was chilly that evening. I sat on the edge of a cedar rail fence listening to crickets. A few ewes came over to watch me watching them. In the distance, I heard the sound of things to come — honking Canada geese circling over a nearby lake where migrating flocks would soon congregate.

And then the ram's lip curled upward, crinkling his nose and revealing his toothless upper gum. Thus self-disfigured, he arched his opened lips skyward and weaved his head back and forth slowly, like a dog wagging its tail on a hot day.

The first time I saw this behaviour I thought something was terribly wrong. Sheep yawn, but this was ridiculous. And it was only the ram doing it. I checked his nostrils for foreign objects, and soon learned that rams, like certain children, do not like to have their noses blown.

Then I called the shepherd who sold me the ram to find out if there was some treatment for the chronic curling of the lip.

Had I done something wrong?

Was the ram in pain? I tried curling my own lip up and found it distinctly uncomfortable, serving no purpose I could possibly think of.

Well, it turns out that the curling lip is all about sex.

Unlike the American President, rams don't try to fool anyone when they are thinking about fooling around. They don't wear silly neckties to send out messages. They just curl their lip and stand there, waggling their heads like goofs.

The lip thing actually has a purpose. Believe it or not, rams have an olfactory sensor in the roof of their mouth. They use this during the breeding season, to check the environment for significant scents regarding the ewes' potential disposition toward mating.

Nothing scandalous about that. Rams don't act on impulse any more than ewes kiss and tell.

I managed to lock the ram in the barn by himself after I saw the lip curl.

I didn't want to interrogate him. That wouldn't do either of us any good. Rather, because I am a good shepherd, I want to make sure that when breeding takes place, it is all aboveboard and all of the animals are in the best condition they can possibly be.

So for the next month or so, the ewes and the ram will receive a special ration of grain. Cisco will not be happy in the barn, no matter what I feed him. In the crisp night air, I will hear his growling *baa* of longing as the sexual tension heightens.

When I decide the time is right, I will strap a leather harness around his chest. It has a large crayon marker fastened to it.

When Cisco is freed to meet his waiting harem, I will walk away from the field of the curling lip and let him do his job.

Unlike the independent prosecutor, Kenneth Starr, I won't need a DNA sample to know what goes on in the privacy of the pasture. The crayon leaves its own evidentiary stain.

Maybe there are things that President Clinton could learn from spending more time with real animals.

Or maybe the American people should be looking for different signs the next time he or any other politician decides to say something such as "Read my lips."

What sheep know to be implicitly true — and what Bill Clinton should have learned long before Ms. Monica curled his lip — is that a good shepherd never betrays the flock.

PUPPY SCHOOL DAYS

Farm dogs have to be sociable and well-behaved to co-exist with livestock and humans ranging from the unannounced hydro-meter-reading person to the uninvited Jehovah's Witnesses, who frequently parade unabashedly up the lane way.

Likewise, farm dog owners can often use some socialization to modify behaviours that result from dealing exclusively with livestock and strangers.

Wally was four months old when we went to puppy school.

"Is that a puppy?" his classmates' owners asked curiously.

Wally was the largest puppy in the class, which consisted largely of younger puppies, limber little puppies and one Jack Russell Terrier the size of a running shoe.

In the meantime, Wally was at that awkward age for a Bull Terrier. His head and his paws seemed huge. His tail wagged his whole body.

"That dog looks like a pig with big feet," one juvenile handler whispered to her mother. Children can be so cruel.

Classes were held in the high-school gymnasium. There were seven pages of introductory notes, starting with an admonition: "This course is a COMMITMENT."

As per instructions, I brought a "puppy mat" with me — a salmon pink carpet remnant that was all I could find at the last minute.

Puppies being puppies, the whole room was in chaos. A Miniature Poodle tried to tear a strip off the Cockapoo. Two Golden Labs ran laps around their owners until their leashes were impossibly tangled. A mixed breed named Griffon kept leaping on a squeaky toy shaped like a fire hydrant that belonged to a very possessive Beagle. At least two puppies peed themselves.

Wally sat there looking miserable. The pink mat was definitely a mistake.

The Instructor strode confidently into the middle of this cacophony of youthful canine enthusiasms accompanied by a black-and-white Border Collie who walked perfectly at his side and sat immediately when he stopped.

Every owner in the room had the same fantasy — simultaneously — My dog: perfectly behaved.

I looked at Wally. He was rolling on his back, chewing on his choke chain.

We worked the puppies for a good half an hour that night, learning to use food treats as "drivers." By the end of the session, some puppies had learned to "sit" on command. We left with homework.

Fall

I learned a lot over the next few weeks. For instance, I learned that expensive dog treats, such as "Snausages," drove Wally to better behaviour than dry doggy biscuits.

Snausages are moist brown jobbies, shaped like cocktail wieners. They come in little tins with snap-off lids. When I first got them, I left them on the kitchen table. The next time I went into the room, there was a jar of mustard sitting beside them, next to an empty beer bottle.

Moose had made a natural mistake.

There were times when Wally seemed to really enjoy himself at puppy school. He liked the "Down" command. When the Instructor came to inspect Wally's progress on that particular exercise, I was determined to do well.

"Down," I announced forcefully, giving Wally a flat-handed hand signal. And down he went. And further down, until he was lying flat on his stomach, back feet splayed, like some kind of large squashed bug.

Then I stood six feet away and gave the "Come" command. Sure enough, Wally began paddling toward me like an army commando — elbows grounded, butt raised.

"At least he understands," the Instructor said, gritting his teeth.

That evening we were given our long leashes. Wally's was lavender.

"I think this instructor has it in for you, Wally," Moose wryly observed.

Teaching Wally to heel took hours of practice.

I walked him beside me as we did the chores, making him sit and stay while I filled buckets of water for the sheep.

I walked him up and down the lane way.

I took him to foreign places, like the supermarket parking lot, and worked him on turning corners with me expertly.

Regardless, Wally always seemed to want to be two steps ahead of me or two steps behind. Snausages weren't working. Wally had so many Snausages he was starting to look like one.

The solution was "pop correction."

I was supposed to give Wally a sudden sharp jerk on his leash every time he was out of step. Thus, the puppy would then learn exactly where he should be in relation to my body to avoid the "pop" he would otherwise receive. I was to look straight ahead, maintain my direction and "pop the pup" whenever I felt he was out of step.

At the beginning of the next class, the Instructor asked me to demonstrate the "pop" heeling process.

"Heel," I commanded, leading off with my left leg as though I were a Polish riding instructor.

Wally was perfectly aligned with me for about ten steps. Then I felt a drag on the leash, so I "popped" him. No response. I "popped" him again and kept moving, even though there seemed to be a dead weight at the end of the leash.

"Oopsie," said the Cockapoo owner, zipping by me with her mop-sized puppy dancing daintily at her side.

"Poopsie," said Griffon's owner, giving me a frazzled look.

I turned to find Wally at the end of his tether, hunched over in the midst of a substantial bowel movement directly beneath the west basketball hoop. His face was etched with distress.

"Clean up," the Instructor shouted.

I didn't "pop" Wally again that night.

The note on the lesson sheet at Week Four said, "Puppies learn at different rates, so please do not get discouraged if your pup is not doing as well as a classmate's pup."

Hah. Make no mistake, life in Puppy School, despite polite appearances to the contrary, is a cut-throat competition.

Sure, I behaved as though I liked the curly-haired black puppy, Griffon, and as though I liked his owner, but, let's face it, Griffon couldn't hold a candle to Wally when it came to doing the "down/stay" exercise.

The Jack Russell did everything perfectly, until he got bored and started attacking his owner's shoe laces.

The Poodle was jumpy.

The Beagle was a barker.

The Golden Labs wriggled.

With a lapse here and there, Wally was perfect. And the test at the end of the course would prove it.

"Your puppy may fail," the Instructor solemnly told the Class at Week Five, "but that is just a sign that you need to do more homework because every puppy can pass."

All owners left the building with a mantra: "I will not fail my puppy, therefore, my puppy will not fail."

Week Six was intense. We entered the gymnasium to find a minefield of puppy temptations.

Bounded by fluorescent highway markers, the basketball court was laden with all manner of puppy toys.

The exercise worked this way: Puppies were expected to sit at one end of the gymnasium while the owner stood at the other end and gave the "Come" command.

Puppies were supposed to stay within the highway markers, ignore the toys and, on the "Come" command, go directly to their owners' side.

Of course, the jumpy black Poodle did it perfectly, treading carefully through the toys and arriving brightly exactly where he was supposed to be. His owner beamed with pride.

I looked at Wally. His eyes were glazed.

Surveying the gymnasium full of doggy toys — stuffed Garfield the Cat toys that meowed when they were chomped by little puppies and colourful plastic squeeze toys in the melt-in-your-mouth shape of hot dogs — he had become unhinged.

There were hard plastic bone-shaped toys, toys that rattled when they moved, and, from Wally's perspective, there was the finest toy of all — a tennis ball.

I kept Wally to the very end, hoping that he would "get it" through a combination of repeated example and osmosis.

Finally it was Wally's turn. A crowd of spectators had gathered at the end of the gym — family members, loved ones and a whole troop of Air Cadets who stopped by after training to watch the puppies.

Then Moose walked in. Wally briefly wagged his tail and then went back to hypnotically staring at the tennis ball.

Wally knew that all eyes were on him. He sat reluctantly, without letting his bottom touch the floor. When I called him, loudly and firmly, he started off in my general direction.

Other class members had given the "Come" command with varying degrees of success but, by-and-large, all the puppies made it to their owners' sides with little fanfare.

It took three full minutes for Wally to finally get to me.

But that was not the worst part.

One of Garfield's legs trailed from his muzzle, where it was lodged between a rattling dog bone and a plastic hot dog. Mashed somewhere in the garbled mess was the bright yellow tennis ball.

In the doorway, Moose lowered his eyes. The Instructor sighed a Saint Bernard-sized sigh. The Jack Russell started pulling on Garfield's leg and Wally finally let go of his treasure trove.

It was then revealed that Wally had also managed to stuff a sock in his mouth.

From that night forward, the Puppy School Test loomed large in front of us, like Mt. Everest. I knew it was going to be a daunting challenge. By the time test day arrived with its majesty and oppressive threat of failure, Wally could stay for a full minute without breaking position.

After the puppy-toy-course fiasco, I literally spent days and nights providing Wally with all manner of distraction.

Sheep walked around him. Cats walked in front of him. Moose yelled things in the background such as "Hamburgers, bacon, bologna, Get your, hamburgers, bacon, bologna."

Through it all, Wally just sat there.

When I called, he came, tail whipping like a helicopter. We were as ready as we were ever going to be.

As anticipated, the Test was torture.

When the Jack Russell broke his down/stay, Griffon's affable owner let out a low growl. The Instructor wove his way through the puppies, a judicious and disgruntled General Patton.

Sometimes he clapped his hand unexpectedly and a puppy would jump toward him unthinkingly. He tossed bags filled with puppy treats past little puppy noses to see if they would budge.

Many did.

When he got to Wally, he suddenly emitted a high-pitched whistle. Nary a twitch.

He waved his arms and shouted, "YOU HOO!"

Wally was bemused but unmoving.

Then came the *coup de grâce*.

The Instructor flipped out a brand new, day-glo yellow, perfectly manufactured tennis ball and gently tossed it toward the centre of the gymnasium.

Wally hit it mid-bounce, projecting it under the Poodle. Result: airborne Poodle.

Still at full tilt, Wally tried to pounce on the ball, which had been propelled by the sheer velocity of his attack into the vicinity of the Golden Labs.

Soon both Lab owners were wrapped in an unintended embrace.

Choosing Wally as a role model, Griffon dashed after the ball too.

The Beagle barked, the Cockapoo peed.

Sensing something run a muck, the Jack Russell chomped on its owner's shoelaces and missed, drawing blood at the ankle.

Wally's lavender long leash trailed after him as the tennis ball careened around the gymnasium as though driven by a McEnroe serve.

I froze in place, until the incident finally ended with the ball trapped behind a bench which had been, blessfully, bolted to the floor.

While the Instructor stood off in a corner grading his scorecards, anxious owners subdued their puppies.

The excitement had been too much for Wally. He promptly fell asleep on his pink mat.

The Instructor called the puppies names, one at a time, a final roll call. He shook their paws and spoke quietly to their masters and mistresses.

Wally stumbled forward, half asleep. When he wouldn't do the paw thing, the Instructor grabbed his foreleg and Wally collapsed in a heap. He looked like I felt.

"Interesting animal," he whispered, and slipped something into my hand.

It was a whole chicken wiener. Wally quickly came to life and inhaled the whole thing.

In the truck, I sat exhausted, while Wally tried to lick Moose's ears.

"How did it go?" he asked.

"He got this," I said, handing him a crumpled ball of paper, which I expected contained a screed about Wally's unsociable Puppy Class *interruptus* behaviour, or lack of behaviour and commitment papers to the nearest Puppy Reform School.

Instead, it was a Graduate Certificate, complete with Wally's name, "Rather's Wallace Stevens," just above my own. It had gilt edges and a little drawing of a Border Collie sitting alertly, as a good dog should.

A note was enclosed. It said: "For best results, limit access to tennis balls."

APPLE ALVIN

You cannot spend half a day with Alvin Filsinger without coming away a more healthy individual. Just keeping up with Alvin is an aerobics exercise, especially if he decides to show you his farm — all 4,000 fruit trees worth, plus the trout pond and the vegetable plots. And, of course, there's that unforgettable compost heap teaming with red-wriggler worms.

The farm is set back from a quiet road just outside of Ayton, Ontario, on gently rolling land. In the barns and assorted outbuildings there are cold-rooms for storage next to the apple-packing room and the juice press.

Somewhere on the place Alvin keeps seventy-five wooden barrels full of apple cider and somewhere else there are twenty bee hives for pollination. If you make the trek all the way to the far side of the property, where a hedge of multiflora roses, thick enough to keep the neighbours' cattle out, rises like heaven on earth for hummingbirds — you start to get a sense of the Filsinger farm, and Alvin himself.

"I had apples in my blood from a kid," Alvin shouted to a couple of dozen organic farming enthusiasts, who had travelled from as far away as Windsor and Hamilton to take a tour of the farm.

At approximately six score and ten years, Alvin has some personal auditory challenges, but it is no problem at all for anyone to hear him.

With a spring in his step that would daunt a Bay Street bond trader half his age, Alvin fairly bounds through his orchards.

Picking his way through a windfall of apples, pointing out sweet red orbs in the grass, he urges those who aspire to organic practices to do the organic thing by eating one.

When he was a boy, Alvin started working on apple trees. There is a McIntosh behind the barn, a few tree rows in, that he started himself.

"It was the first week of May, 1937, and I asked my dad and my uncle to teach me how to graft a tree," he says, sidling up to a gnarl-limbed tree laden with fruit.

The tree in question was a transplanted wild sapling with a trunk about an inch thick at the time. Alvin describes his elders using frying pans coated with beeswax to prepare the McIntosh graft. He knows exactly where he put it, and he remembers the cow that chewed a bit off the crown of the growing grafted tree. Then he's off again.

Not just McIntosh grows in his orchard — there are early apples, mid-season and late apples. Some of his root stock is of Russian origin — winter-hardy, Siberian crab apple trees.

He has Yellow Harvest apples, Empires, Spys, scab-resistant Liberty apple trees and dwarf Joni-golds that boast apples the size of George Chuvalo's fist.

If you get tired of apple trees, he has plum trees and pear trees and rows of grapevines in another spot.

Some of his apples end up in tidy cardboard palettes for shipping to commercial supermarkets. These are what Alvin calls "the pretty stuff." Pesticide free, chemical free, unadulterated apples picked at the height of their sweetness according to Alvin's scientific tool called a refracameter, and his own unerring sense of all that is apple.

But most of Alvin's apples end up as sauce, or juice, butter, vinegar or cider because according to Alvin "the public is getting harder to satisfy. If there is a bump on an apple, people don't think it is good. Today, everybody wants picture-perfect fruit."

If you ask Alvin why that is, he might just tell you that it's because "the human beings did not take care of things."

The way he sees it, the mass of big red apples on produce counters that weren't allowed to hang on the tree long enough to earn the sweetness of their appearance are, likely as not, never eaten to the core.

"Kids only take about six bites of a big store-bought apple," he declares. "By then they've started to fill up and they know it doesn't taste too good."

But Alvin does not dwell on the dark side of non-organic food. That he leaves to the individual, although if you press him about the processing of modern food, he is just as likely to pull back on his suspenders and say something like, "The whiter the bread, the sooner you're dead." And then he marches on.

Alvin is big on compost. Bits of pruned tree branches and twigs litter the floor of the orchard, along with cut grass that mulches naturally.

"Here," he says, bending over suddenly and coming up with a handful of black guck. "Smell this — that's biodynamics for you. Biodynamic people love that smell." Then he points to the place the guck came from, and shouts with glee, "And look at all those worms."

Politely, the organic enthusiasts lean toward the dark clump and, sure enough, a few earth worms struggle to find a hole away from their hole.

Alvin calls his farm a research centre. He has been farming organically since 1953. He has battled gnawing mice, coddling moths and the dreaded oblique leaf roller with everything from blackstrap molasses to soya oil emulsions and tricgrama wasps.

"I'm learning all the time," he told the weary marchers in organic soil, as we trudged across a knee-high alfalfa field beside rows of lush carrot-tops flagging in the breeze over their foot-long orange roots.

Fall

Back at the store, where Alvin sells everything from juicers to books about juice and puff balls and spaghetti squash and garlic, the organic wannabee entourage paused to catch their breath.

Then anxious shoppers buzzed around the store, filling up their plain paper bags with packages of buckwheat and brown rice. Juicers were crammed into trunks and vans for the gas-guzzling journey home.

The fall air was heavy with the smell of apples. Alvin was standing off in a corner, looking across the lane at a field full of fruit-laden trees waiting to be picked. All the while, his gnarled fingers beat a gentle rhythm on the shiny skins of a bushel of apples at his side. He looked like a man with apples in his blood.

MIRACLE ON MAIN STREET

Drive through almost any small town these days and you will see vacant storefronts. You will also see storefronts that have clearly been occupied by the same business for years. Then there are the storefronts with spanking new signs — those are stores occupied by either the bravest, most naive or the dimmest entrepreneurs in the world.

Starting a new business, particularly a retail business, is a risky enterprise anywhere. In a small town, anyone who opens shop is well-advised to have a long line of ancestors buried in the local cemetery and a heap of prosperous cousins who are active in the local service clubs.

When I first moved to the country, I fearlessly explored every new shop in every nearby town. A new shop opened and I would march right in. After a while, I began to wonder why I never saw anyone else in these testaments to mankind's capacity for hope in the face of insurmountable odds.

When talking with neighbours I began to notice that they would often ask me if I had been into such-

and-such a shop yet. When I answered in the affirmative I would be prodded for a detailed description of inventory and a list of the prices.

Six months later, I would discover it was all for naught because the new store had closed.

It took me years to understand what was going on.

Like the first Mennonite who ever wore a zipper, I had been breaking an ancient rule of conduct.

My transgression did not stop the curious locals from wanting to know what the experience was like. After all, I could be excused. I didn't know any better. I was from "away."

The rule in question is the one that prohibits anyone from going into any new shop or patronizing any new business for at least six months, with a few exceptions. For example, if you are collecting rent or carrying the child of the proprietor, you would be exempt.

If a new business somehow miraculously survives the six-month rule, a trickle of customers gradually begin to tentatively tiptoe onto the premises.

This provokes talk in the coffee shop, and plenty of reminiscence about whatever business was there before and how much it is missed, but the locals will gradually start patronizing the joint.

Prices are pressure points. A new restaurant once opened in a town I frequent. A month or so later, the woman who manages the convenience store where I buy the newspaper asked me if I had eaten there yet. I allowed I hadn't.

"Well," she said in a conspiratorial whisper, "They're selling potato skins with cheese — for $3.95! How long can you stay in business doing that?"

Good question. How long, indeed?

I started hearing about those pricey potato skins everywhere I went.

Since then, the restaurant has changed ownership three times in three years.

The first thing everyone does when they see a new name on the sign is ask someone they suspect may have eaten there since it changed hands whether there are potato skins on the menu.

"There aren't? The cook is married to a local girl, you say? Who would that be? The owner coaches pee-wee hockey?"

With certain conditions finally met, this incarnation of the restaurant has an odds-on chance to survive.

If a new business owner/operator "comes from away," it is crucial that they establish some timely or long-lost link to the community. Any straw is worth a grab.

One relative who served in an army battalion that even one ancient Legionnaire still remembers creates an instant, *bona fide* connection.

If your mother's brother married the 1962 Dairy Princess and they still visit the family farm at Easter, someone will think they know who you are talking about. If all else fails, it will be necessary to marry someone who is related to the Mayor or change your name to Tim Horton.

Even with the endurance and nepotic conditions satisfied, new businesses often have to be diverse operations. Hence, you will often find interesting retail combinations under the same roof.

Photo-finishing and framing is a natural enough link to something like book selling, but pets and video rentals is something else: "Specials Today: New Schwarzenegger blockbuster/ Ragdoll Kittens Ready to Go."

Overnight successes are as rare on Main Street as in Hollywood. I have only witnessed one, and it put the lie to another enduring myth of country life in the process.

In my 20 or so years on the farm I have seen things and been told many stories. The old adage that one sees the damnest things when unarmed has stood the test of time.

However, the most persistent falsehood, the most overweaning myth surrounds the idea that there is actually something called "good ol' down-home country cookin'."

The proprietors of the new business that illuminated this impenetrable secret for me were not only from out of town, they had immigrated from the big city with no blood ties, or anything.

Fall

Then they had the unmitigated gall to buy a building on Main Street that once housed one of the most popular beauty parlours in town.

The beauty parlour's demise caused such an enduring wave of discombobulation that certain ladies still inadvertently walk into the store expecting to see Adele and get a perm. They often become thoroughly disoriented when they see loaves of bread rather than hair rinse products on the shelves.

Worse, these urban interlopers planned to open a bakery in a community where baking cakes and cookies was not only a ritual, it was a sacred right.

The rural countryside, according to the myth, is the home of "country cooking," an enduring symbol of family values, goodness and light.

In such a landscape, people know how to peel a potato within an inch of its life, and they can incorporate a marshmallow into anything from a fruit salad to a cream pie.

The actual fact is that anything involving the joining of the words "country" and "cooking" should be avoided at all costs.

The worst examples are found at events billed as "suppers." These are invariably hosted by a church group, civic organizations or local clubs.

They may be touted as "fowl suppers" or "roast beef suppers," but whenever a food classification is followed by the word "supper" and the address is rural, my best advice is to opt out by booking a medical procedure that entitles you to an official paper stating that you must *fast* for at least 12 hours.

It is not that country people do not like to eat. They do. These suppers are prime examples of that. They will eat anything that is put upon their plate and declare it delicious, even when it is unknown grey meat topped with a gelatinous substance of questionable origin. Chicken, pork or beef might be mixed up on a plate, but one gravy serves all.

With gusto, those who attend these suppers welcome what are hailed as mashed potatoes, usually identifiable by their lumps.

The whole mess is surrounded with khaki and rust-coloured vegetables, topped with some limp, sweetened cabbage and a dill pickle the texture of liver.

Then there is the matter of dessert.

At most suppers, there is an early "buzz" about pies.

It is almost guaranteed that any cherry pie served in March involved someone opening a can of cherry-pie filling.

The "homemade" designation is derived from the fact that someone purchased a frozen pie shell into which they poured a tin's contents and took responsibility for the hydro bill necessary to bake it.

Anything covered in meringue has something related to Jello underneath.

Nevertheless, there is seldom a flake of pastry left in the building when any supper is over.

Why? Any pies that remain at the formal end of the supper are invariably set on the long, wrapping, paper-covered industrial tables. Then they are set upon and devoured as though they were the last pies on earth.

"Country cooking" seems to be more about quantity than quality. Why else would people stand in line to heap their plates with huge slabs of perfectly good meat that has been cooked into something the taste and texture of corrugated cardboard. But, by golly, it's a tradition that belongs to country people and is inextricably linked to the collective sense of identity.

When city folk want a good meal, they go out to eat. Country folk go home.

When city people dine out, they eat food that is most often prepared by well-schooled men wearing starched white hats who care deeply about things like ingredients and presentation.

Country people eat what's on their plate.

Upstart urbanites, who come from a world where words like "gastronomic delight" and "culinary experience" are dished out along with double-digit priced appetizers, are not welcomed. Crème brûlée doesn't cut it at the coffee shop stolid rice pudding with a few whacked out raisins does. That is why I was certain that a bakery founded on urban principles would never succeed.

Other bakeries had tried and closed. Two supermarkets sell baked goods and there's a Tim Horton's at the crossroads. And then there's the perennial buga-boo of price point.

Jeannette and Doug, the couple who started the Village Bakery, knew nothing of these things about which I speak. If they had, they certainly would not have done what they did.

Hale and handsome mid-life folk embarking on a second career in what they thought was a quaint, quiet, beautiful small town (one, surprisingly, with-out a bakery), they earnestly began renovating their shop on Main Street.

When I say they lived their business as it took shape, I mean it literally — in the two storeys above the shop.

Two years after the Village Bakery had opened, I picked up my Thanksgiving order.

It was a good thing I had called a day ahead because the bread racks were bare by the time I got there in the mid-afternoon.

Every pumpkin torte had been spoken for. Every last crumb of the best cranberry and blueberry pound cake ever to come out of a loaf pan was boxed and labelled for pickup. Doug told me he could have sold everything twice.

It has miraculously been like that ever since the bakery opened.

But their success was not the result of something as ebullient as a complicated strategic marketing plan. It was, in its way, pure genius and a business lesson for anyone who might care to pay attention. It was impulsive, sincere and deceptively simple.

Being from the city, and children of their age, Jeannette and Doug took cooking seriously and knew something about it from books. But they had no hands-on experience.

While figuring out the craft of baking, testing recipes and searching out the best combinations for the finest ingredients, they often ended up with a surplus of experimental product.

"We gave the stuff away where we thought it would be most welcomed and useful," laughs Doug, a jovial former commercial photographer, whose specialty today is making round loaves of spinach, garlic and cheese bread that have to be eaten to be believed.

Loaves of flax bread fresh from the oven found their way to the hospital cafeteria — for the staff.

Pans full of double-chocolate killer brownies were dropped off at the police station which just happened to be a regional centre. That meant about three hundred uniformed and well-armed men with spouses and families in the immediate vicinity had an exclusive preview of Jeannette's and Doug's wizardry.

Not knowing any better, Jeannette even went so far as to accost Town Councillors in their cars at the stoplight outside the shop, thrusting butter tarts through their window.

"Let me know what you think," she'd say.

What did they think?!?

First, they thought, what cheek! I don't know that person.

Then they thought, Holy smokes, free stuff.

Then, Hmmm, hmmm good.

Then they realized that their spouses, their mothers and sisters really had never really known how to bake anything, and from that day forward insisted that the family start buying all their pies, cakes and bread at that new bakery by the library,

"What's it called, Town Bakery or Village Bakery? Nevermind. It's right there just north of the Town Hall. You can't miss it."

Even badly baked cookies can be addictive. Great baking can blow the mind.

And boy, did Jeannette and Doug's ever do just that.

When the "OPEN" sign finally appeared, without any fanfare or hoopla, customers came in droves.

In fact, opening day was one of the biggest Jeannette and Doug have ever had.

"Townies" and farm folk found themselves stacked side-by-side in front of the bakery, waiting their turn and admiring a fanciful collection of cookie jars that perch on a shelf above the bread racks. Price became no object.

People were paying more for one of Jeannette's pies than they would ever consider coughing up for a whole "supper." I've never heard a word about price in relation to the Village Bakery.

A little cartoon on the cash register about sums it up:

One image shows a pie on a table with the sign, "Mom's apple pie: $2." Next to it is the same table with a better looking pie. The sign reads, "The pie Mom thought she baked: $5."

It does the heart good to see a new business in a small town achieve its goals and add a new dimension to the community.

"I need a good pie," I overheard an elderly lady lean into the counter and whisper to Doug the other day. With a twinkle in her eye and the demeanour of an experienced bargainer, she added, "It's for the church supper,"

"Oh, we've sold lots of pies for that supper, dear," chirped Jeannette, as she emerged from the back room with a tray of three lattice-work encrusted beauties fresh from the oven.

The old lady handed Doug the money without further comment and hurried out of the store. I suspect that pie never made it to any church supper. I doubt it even made it to dinner time.

THAT CHAMPIONSHIP SEASON

While the farmers were taking off the second cut of hay and worrying about rain, I was putting makeup on my dog and worrying about rain. Go figure. I was going to a dog show.

At sheep shows, I have seen that it takes a fair amount of primping to make a sheep a champion. Fluff the wool a little here, trim it back a little there — use a black felt-tip marker to disguise a few white hairs where there should be only black. In dire straits, go for the Miss Clairol.

Cattle breeders use vacuums and hair blowers on their prize beef. They have trunks full of clippers and hair shiners, hair spray and hoof gloss. And, I hate to tell you this, but there was a scandal in the dairy industry when certain competitors were accused of enhancing the udders of prize-winning cows with silicon injections.

People will go to ungodly lengths to try and win a silly ribbon. That notion really struck home for me when I found myself wiping a cosmetic sponge covered with clown makeup over Wally the Wonder Dog's gigantic nose.

It started innocently enough. A few Bull Terrier owners complimented Wally's good looks and said he had "show potential."

That was some solace to me, since he had shown no sheep-herding potential. Lambs stamp their hooves at him and he runs away — at top speed, usually aiming for my knees. He tries to engage the horses by squatting in front of them and wagging his tail like a helicopter ready for take-off. They just snort in his general direction. He's good at chasing chickens across rows of round bales of hay, disrupting the stacking of anything, and jumping into puddles.

"Show potential" sounded soothing.

It took a year for me to figure out how to enter Wally in a dog show. When I told his dog-obedience instructor what I was planning, I was dispatched to a store that specializes in dog show equipment, where I could find fancy, thin, show leashes and a chain so fine it could be a silver necklace.

There were aisles chock-a-block with doggy things, everything from life-sized plastic fire hydrants to bags full of those impossibly tiny little bows people use to hold the hair out of the eyes of furry little lap dogs. There was even a special counter for pet perfume and hygiene aids, including "whitening, brightening" toothpaste to go with curved canine toothbrushes.

Dog foods ran the gamut from puppy to geriatric, with all manner of gummy bone, raw hide bone and fake salami in between. Then there was what must be the ultimate in the waste-not-want-not category — dried pigs' ears.

Real late-pigs' hearing devices dried to a crisp for Fido's pleasure.

Perhaps that explains the toothpaste.

Before I could grab a shopping cart, Moose bagged the fine chain and leash and whisked me out of the store, muttering something about turning Wally into some kind of "girly dog."

On the day of the dog show I got out the garden hose and gave Wally a bath. I brushed him until he shone and clipped his toenails. That was it, I thought. Ready for the show. I had a fresh package of something called Beggin' Bacon to make Wally stand prettily and my secret weapon — a lacrosse ball.

I was totally unprepared for what greeted me at the arena that day. A thousand dogs of every variety imaginable stared out of metal cages, plastic dog houses and little pens. There were trailers and vans filled with dogs in the parking lot. In one corner of the arena, huge Old English Sheepdogs stood on sturdy stands while their personal groomers worked the hair dryers. Scissors and shears trimmed Poodles in some sort of art form, while every silky strand of Lhasa Apso was carefully combed in place. Impossibly tiny bows were everywhere.

Moose thought taking Wally to a dog show was the biggest waste of time I had come up with since trying to get chickadees to take seed from my hand in the winter. We waded through a sea of dogs and dog owners before reaching the ring just as the Bull Terrier class was called. I examined Wally. His paws were still white.

Having watched a few dog shows on satellite television, I had some idea of the routine. My numbered armband was adjusted and I swung into the ring with Wally. He was perfect. Trotted around looking joyful. Stopped dead still like an alert statue when I pulled out the lacrosse ball. The judge patted his body and, at the appropriate moment, Wally looked deeply into the judge's eyes and wagged his tail. What showmanship!

Wally won a ribbon. It was unreal. We kept going back in the ring and winning some more. In the end, Wally got a trophy and a handful of Beggin' Bacon. Moose was jumping up and down like a bee-stung goat. I shook the limp hands of the losers and realized that these were professional dog handlers. Wally the Wonder Dog had emerged from nowhere and ruined their day.

Alas, we never regained our early glory.

The professionals always topped us in the final round. It was going to be a long limp toward winning the title of champion.

Moose started developing conspiracy theories, drawing charts showing which judges favoured what handler and griping about American dogs stealing the thunder of Canadian dogs.

Once, when Wally seemed sure to take the top prize, we were called into the judging ring at the precise moment that a neighbouring dog had what would be called a rather large "accident."

"Clean up," shouted the professional handler without a hint of embarrassment.

I looked at Wally. His almost-champion face was a twisted grimace that said, "Somebody's in a lot of trouble." It was the same look he gave the Basset-faced judge. Then he tried to hide from sight by burying his head under her skirt.

"Control your dog," she commanded.

Wally looked up.

Moose added that judge to his list of conspirators.

Our final show was an outdoor extravaganza that promised to bring out the *crème de la crème* of dogdom. Wally was ready in spirit, but not in form.

By mid-summer, he had developed a fair-sized callus on his nose from heading off soccer balls. Then he chased a chipmunk into a woodpile, adding splinter wounds to go with whatever damage a cornered groundhog can do.

Bluntly put, Wally's nose was a bloody mess of bumps, bruises and scabs.

I thought of forfeiting the entry fee. Then I remembered how things work in sheep shows and cattle shows. I checked with a friend who is an old hand in the world of doggy showing and discovered that the remedy for Wally's nose was clown-white makeup and a dusting of corn starch.

Where in a small town in southwestern Ontario was I going to find clown makeup? Stedman's, of course.

Sure enough, there on the toy rack facing the vegetable peelers and potato mashers, I found a tube of clown-white Halloween makeup, non-toxic to children. Stedman's never lets you down.

Applying makeup to a teenaged Bull Terrier is not an easy matter. By the time I finished, my arms were streaked with clown white, and a whole section of the kitchen floor was covered in a fine dusting of corn starch.

Moose surveyed my handiwork.

"He looks like a girl," was the verdict.

On the drive to the dog show, Wally rolled in the back seat. When we arrived, the upholstery was clown white.

I registered, leaving Moose to exercise Wally. When I found them, they were in the middle of a crowd of children putting on a show of their own.

"Batter up!" Moose cried. Then he lobbed a tennis ball at Wally, who promptly hit it back with his nose. More clown white was applied. Dusted in corn starch, I looked more like Bela Lugosi than any show-ring belle.

Spectators in lawn chairs lined the show rings.

Chihuahua owners carried their dogs in vest pockets to keep them from disappearing in patches of long grass.

A Yorkshire Terrier passed by, carried aloft as though it was a stuffed toy.

Elegant Afghans paused to have their paws groomed before stepping daintily into the ring.

Apparently sensing the odds of an "accident" occurring in such a large number of dogs, Wally commenced howling and barking.

Reluctantly, he followed me into the show ring, squirming to check out the dogs behind him.

Then a child on the sidelines shouted, pointing at Wally: "Mom, it's the dog that hits balls with his nose!"

Wally heard the word "ball" and promptly went into a crouch waiting for the games to begin. I tried to straighten him out and instead he flopped down on all fours.

I looked down the row of dogs. Professional handlers in tweed suits held skinny leashes over still-as-stone, perk-eared Bull Terriers.

"Round the ring," said the judge.

Wally lurched to his feet. The idea is for the dog to show off his gaits. But Wally was having none of it. He wanted to sniff the grass for underground moles before he took another step. Behind us, a line of dogs jogged in place like finely tuned dressage horses.

Wally jitterbugged all over the ring somewhere between a trot and a gallop. He jumped in the air and kicked out his hind legs. The crowd loved it, especially when the leash became tangled around my leg, and Wally barked while I twirled around, trying to free myself.

With an arch of his finger, the judge called us for inspection. Beads of sweat formed on my brow, sunglasses hung askew.

"Teeth, please," said the judge. I wrested Wally's jaws open, revealing a Beggin' Bacon strip glued to his incisors.

The judge patted Wally's head and a cloud of corn starch poofed in his face.

At the tail end of the examination, the judge tried to check Wally's breeding equipment. Wally suddenly reared back and gave the judge such a look as though to say, "What the hell do you think you're doing, you pervert?"

"To the corner," said the judge curtly. I felt as though I was tugging an anchor. I went the wrong way.

"Miss, diagonal, please," called the judge. I turned too suddenly and tripped. Wally stopped my fall by jamming his head in my face, followed by a full body licking.

"You two are a pair, aren't you?" noted the judge.

We waited in line while the other dogs performed beautifully. My nose was bleeding. Nothing a make-up sponge covered in clown's white makeup couldn't absorb.

Bored, Wally decided to dig a hole, apparently to China.

To distract him and spare the spectators from flying clods of dirt, I pulled out his favourite thing in the entire word — the lacrosse ball.

Bingo, he butted it out of my hand where it rolled under the belly of an American bred Bull Terrier whose owner had travelled half a continent to see his dog win a ribbon. The Yankee dog lunged backward in an unseemly fashion. So did the judge, whose heel slipped on the ball, propelling him into the lap of a large lady who may have had a Chihuahua in her vest pocket.

We did not win that day. By some miracle, Wally placed third. The crowd applauded. I wiped my brow, smearing clown white across my forehead.

"Looking more and more like your dog, Miss," said the judge when he handed me the ribbon. "Pervert," I thought.

That was the end of Wally's career as a show dog.

Outside of the ring, Moose took Wally on a tour of the grounds. Man and dog trotted in a straight line.

A crowd of children gathered and Wally shot tennis balls off his nose until it started to rain.

Our makeup melted and that was fine with Moose. I went back to worrying about that second cut of hay, and Wally went back to soccer and searching the barnyard for moles.

ANOTHER ROADSIDE ATTRACTION

How the cow got the pail stuck on her head will always be a mystery. What is known is that it was a rather large metal pail. Somehow the handle became lodged in the cow's mouth like a horse's bit, while the bucket itself was firmly lodged over her horns. This combination effectively blinded and enraged the brown cow, who was known as "Betty."

Cattle can behave in irrational ways without any complicating factors. As a heifer, Betty had stolen into an orchard and consumed an idiotic quantity of apples which nearly killed her.

After the birth of her first calf, she seemed to develop a modicum of cow sensibility, behaving as part of the herd and seldom drawing attention to herself.

Unlike dairy cows, who are milked twice a day and regularly enjoy human contact, Betty was a beef cow. Her sole purpose was to create new cows for human consumption. She did not know this or she might have become enraged much earlier. Instead,

Betty plodded through life and seemed happiest of all when she was out standing in a summer field swatting her tail around and licking the calf standing at her side.

The first person to discover Betty wearing the pail was a passing motorist. He was driving by the Hadley farm when he noticed a gaping hole in the straight, white wooden fence. Betty was swinging her head in the ditch. The rest of the herd kept its distance, as if severing themselves from this unusual event.

Mr. Caldwell knew nothing about cows. He sold business forms and rarely came close to anything resembling a farm. Still, he stopped his car and rolled down the window. Betty heard a rumbling in the gravel at the edge of the road and charged toward it, bumping her knee on the bumper of Mr. Caldwell's blue Ford Escort.

A pickup truck was coming in the opposite direction. Mr. Caldwell waved his arm out the window and started honking his horn to warn the driver. Freaked, blind Betty swerved into the roadway.

Earl Rapp saw the whole thing coming and slowly pulled his pickup truck across from Mr. Caldwell.

"Best to stay in your car, Mister," Earl told Mr. Caldwell, who had no intention of getting anywhere except out of there.

"I know, it already attacked me," shouted Mr. Caldwell.

Fall

Earl didn't believe that, but he did know that a cow with a pail stuck on its head in the middle of the road was an unpredictable predicament. Betty had worked herself into quite a sweat. Her mouth was agape. She kept trying to spit out the metal — to no avail. At the sound of the men's voices she flicked her head, took four steps sideways and stumbled into the opposite ditch, where she slipped on some wet grass and landed on her rump.

"What's it doing now?" Mr. Caldwell asked, leaning out the window.

"Just having a sit down," said Earl. "You stay here and I'll get some help. And don't honk your horn, just flick your lights. Okay?"

Earl found John Hadley working on his tractor.

"Hate to tell you this, John, but you've got a cow with a pail on its head sitting in the ditch by the side of the road back there," Earl announced.

John absorbed the information. His lower lip rose to the base of his nose and his teeth chattered.

"I'm coming," he said, tossing his tool box into the back of his pickup truck. As he drove out of the lane way he told his wife to call the neighbours.

"Tell them we may need a hand with a runaway," he said. "And maybe someone should bring a gun, just in case."

A gun was just what Mr. Caldwell had in mind when he saw the cow lurching toward his car after laboriously lifting herself from the ditch.

"There's a mad cow with a pail on its head out on Sideroad Two. It just attacked my car and now it's coming back," he shouted into his cellular phone.

"You might want to get out there, sir," said the police dispatch officer on the other end of the line.

"But it's right in front of me," cried Mr. Caldwell.

Betty followed the sound of his voice and the pail clanged against the hood of the car.

"Arrgh," was the last sound the dispatcher heard. The cow rammed the vehicle with such force that it knocked the phone out of Mr. Caldwell's sweaty grip and sent it flying into the roadway.

Earl and John approached the scene slowly, driving on opposite sides of the soft-shouldered road, hazard lights flashing. Mr. Caldwell had rolled up his window and climbed into the backseat of his car, where he pressed his face into the back window shouting something that could not be heard, which was probably best.

Betty walked uncomfortably on the roadway and nearly slipped when her front hoof skidded on the shattered cell phone. Mr. Caldwell pressed his hands to his ears and slumped into the backseat.

John Hadley recognized the cow and immediately understood how stressful and potentially dangerous this situation was to Betty. He rolled down his window and tried talking to her.

"Soo boss, soo boss," he crooned in a low gentle voice. John had no idea where the phrase "soo boss" came from, but he had been using it all his life whenever he wanted his cattle to feel some measure of comfort.

He would certainly have used it on Betty when she was straining to give birth or when he was moving cattle from one pen to another in the barn. The brown cow lowered her head, sides heaving, and she listened.

"Thing would be to try to get her back in the field," Earl Rapp called across the roadway in an even voice.

John nodded and both men gently nudged the doors of their trucks open. They were just beginning their approach when three of the Daillard boys pulled up in their truck and the youngest idiot started shouting.

"Heard you had a cow loose, what can we do for you," shouted Ned Daillard, the youngest of the well-known, semi-demented clan of pig farmers.

Betty whirled toward the unfamiliar voice, sending a spray of cow slobber across the driver's side window of Mr. Caldwell's shiny new blue car. He glared out at her through the green-foam spittle as though she were an alien.

John and Earl motioned the Daillard crew to stay quiet. More trucks arrived, lining the road-edge as they do at auctions.

Earl then moved over to John's truck, which was roughly established as headquarters, and farmers crept silently along the edge of the ditch to confer on the tailgate. In the distance, there was the sound of a siren.

Passing traffic was neighbourly about stopping for the cow. But Mrs. Betelmayer was bound and determined to get her school bus through come hell or high water. She nudged the bus along in first gear, while the kids pressed their noses to the windows and giggled.

As expected, Betty moved away from the sound and the fumes of the school bus. The brown cow banged her knee on Mr. Caldwell's front bumper. She appeared to be heading awkwardly back into the ditch leading to her pasture when the bus back-fired, sending a ton of unground hamburger straight up in the air like a rodeo bull.

"Whoa," someone on the tailgate cried, and blind Betty ran toward the voice.

Men scattered, leaping into the backs of their trucks. Mrs. Betelmayer shifted into second and pulled away. Betty shook her pail covered head and zig-zagged along the centre of the road.

The police cruiser pulled up a safe enough distance away, with its lights flashing to alert any other traffic. Constable McIntee had grown up on a farm and he had enough sense to adopt a "wait and see attitude."

The men were trying to figure out how to get close enough to the cow to tie a hobbling rope to her back legs, so they could immobilize her while they snipped the pail handle with long-handled, metal shears. In theory, once the cow could see, she could be herded back to where she belonged without incident.

Unbeknownst to anyone, 14-year-old Amanda Hadley had exited the school bus and headed directly for the scene. Constable McIntee was the first one to spot the slight, blond teenager running through the long grass. Grown men taking their chances with a crazed cow was one thing, but the Constable wasn't one to allow a child to be at risk.

Although he had never had occasion to draw his weapon in more than 20 years of serving and protecting his community, Constable McIntee showed no fear when he opened his cruiser window and fired a shot into the air. Once deafened, the air grew still.

"There's a kid behind you," he shouted in the general direction of John Hadley and the rest.

Betty was fear-frozen by the blast. And it was all quite too much for Mr. Caldwell, who crawled back into the front seat of his car and purposefully fastened his seat belt.

At the roadside, John Hadley whisked Amanda into the back of his pickup truck with one sweep of his strong right arm. She was crying.

"Did he shoot her, dad, did he?" she asked in a panicky whisper.

"Naw, just be quiet, stay down and don't move," John told Amanda. But she persisted.

"That's Betty, my Wilford's mother, I know her," said Amanda. "She'll come to me and Wilford, no matter what. Don't let them shoot her."

Wilford was Betty's most recent calf, and when he had been weaned he became Amanda's 4H calf. On any given day after school, Amanda and Wilford practised walking together as they would in a show ring, him responding to her gentle tug on his white and green calf halter. At 600 pounds, Wilford was hardly a "baby," but when Amanda brushed his coat she always tied him next to the pasture, where he could nuzzle his mother. Betty would lean her head through the wood slats on the fence to lick him.

"She knows me, dad," Amanda said in an echo of the same forceful tone her mother used when she was making a point.

In his car, Mr. Caldwell watched the cow zig-zagging in his direction. He turned on his windshield wipers and tried to clear the slowly drying cow slobber.

The *whish, whoosh* of the wipers attracted Betty and she stumbled toward the blue Ford. Four steps later, Mr. Caldwell fired up the ignition and grabbed the steering wheel. Betty turned away when she heard the roll of the tires. She snorted and trotted in what she thought was the opposite direction. Ramming into Constable McIntee's cruiser was not intentional.

The cruiser door swung open, blocking Mr. Caldwell's escape route.

With his gun drawn, Constable McIntee posi-
tioned himself behind the door. In his first-ever, Clint
Eastwood moment, the police officer was facing
down a cow with a pail stuck over her head.

"I've got her in my sights," shouted Ned Daillard,
who was crammed into the front seat of his father's
pickup truck with two of his brothers, all of them bearing arms ranging from a .22 – 250 varmint rifle to a 16
guage shotgun and a 50 lb crossbow. Alec Daillard
made a heap of noise when he dropped the crossbow
out of the back window into the truck cab, and then got
himself stuck trying to squeeze through the window.

Betty broadsided the Daillard truck, denting the
door and scraping off a swath of red paint.

Alec waved like a sock on a clothesline in the back
window, while his brothers tried to haul him back in.

"Y'all wait right there," shouted John Hadley,
cupping his hands into a megaphone. He swung his
truck into the roadway and headed back to the farm.

"Don't shoot, don't shoot!" shouted Ned Daillard,
when he saw that Constable McIntee had turned his
weapon on the cow that was now leaning unsteadily
against the truck door.

Without a "clear shot" Constable McIntee stepped
back into his cruiser, motioning Mr. Caldwell to stay
calm and shut off his windshield wipers.

Betty backed away from the Daillard truck, nudg-
ing her hind end against Constable McIntee's trunk,
where she deposited a moist cow-pie, and sighed

audibly. The Daillards rolled up their windows, so did Constable McIntee.

From the Hadley farm lane way it was a good quarter mile. John Hadley was slowly backing his truck and livestock van down the middle of the road, while everyone watched and wondered what was coming next.

He got as close as he could and pulled to a stop, motioning for Earl Rapp to join him. At the back of the trailer, the two men opened the door and adjusted the ramp as quietly as they could. Inside the two-stall van, Amanda was holding Wilford by his halter.

The calf was a redder shade of brown than his mother and his long tail had a flaxen tip.

Wilford backed out of the van noisily, and John Hadley took the rope lead from his daughter and told her to get in the truck. Standing in the centre of such focused attention, Wilford bawled as if on cue.

Betty knew that voice.

"Soo boss, soo boss," called John and he walked the calf toward its mother, singing the words softly, hoping the cow would pick up the sound of her son's advancing hoof-steps.

But Wilford stopped when he saw the cow with the pail on its head. Mother or not, this was one strange sight, not to mention the flashing lights on the police cruiser.

"Gee haw!" Amanda's voice rang out. "Gee haw, Wilf, gee haw!" Betty knew that voice, too.

Fall

When mother and son finally inched close enough together to hear each other's breathing, Earl moved in with the metal clipper.

Later, John Hadley said it was like watching an owl pluck a rabbit out of a field. So fast and so smooth, it was over before old Betty realized what happened.

With a lick of her thick pink tongue Betty had the handle out her mouth and the pail tilted to one side, allowing her to see Wilford out of one eye. He touched his nose on hers, and she moved forward to lick his neck as she had ever since he was born. John came around to remove the pail, and she paid him no mind.

For a minute or two, people just looked on. Amanda joined her father and took Wilford's rope. She led him down the ditch and into the pasture, with his mother following like the contented cow she had been before the pail got stuck on her head. Engines were started, and the Daillards unlocked and unloaded.

At the edge of the road, Mr. Caldwell finally gave up on trying to recover pieces of his cell phone.

John Hadley asked him if he wanted to come back to the farm to use the phone there, maybe stay for supper considering what he'd been through. But Mr. Caldwell was determined to put as much distance as possible between himself and anything to do with cows. He kicked the pail into the ditch and took off.

Constable McIntee pulled himself to his full height and accepted John's offer of the use of his garden hose on the cruiser. He was glad things had worked out. Still, he would have to file a report since he had fired his weapon. John assured him that all the witnesses present could be called on to verify that he acted in the line of duty.

At school the next day, Amanda was hailed as a heroine. When she took Wilford to the fall fair, there was applause for them even before they won first prize.

Betty grew round and prepared to deliver another calf.

She never went near a metal pail again.

Winter

MAILBOX JUSTICE

When the township announced plans to widen the road in front of my farm so that it could accommodate two lanes of traffic comfortably, I just had one question.

"What happens to my mailbox?"

The box itself did not concern me, just the placement of its new post.

For many years, I have been lugging my mailbox up and down the lane way every day, setting it on its post an hour before Len the Mailman delivers and picking it up early in the afternoon.

This exercise was predicated by sporadic outbursts of mailbox murder. This is a ritual form of rural slaughter that often results in the residents of an entire concession awakening to find that their mailboxes have been bruised, battered or lopped off by young hooligans armed with baseball bats or tire irons.

As customs go, it is a primitive form of self-expression, which, I am led to understand, generally passes when the perpetrators master the art of shaving.

As crimes go, at least the immediate victim feels no pain. And the irritant to the owner is the same whether the fallen mailbox is the consequence of vandals or, as has happened far too often in my township, a snowplough operator runs amok in a new, unfamiliar machine.

However, there is something about mailbox murders that people take very personally. Firstly, very often the crime tends to be a serial one. A dozen people along a single concession road may awake to the horror of felled mailboxes.

Secondly, mailboxes are alone and defenceless and, although we love them less when they hold bills, we cherish the notion far more than any urban-dweller of cheques in them and private missives from the loved or the long-lost. E-mail and voice mail will never replace the intimacy of real mail.

I have heard many a tale about mailboxes missing in action. In fact, you can usually count on a story about a mauled mailbox anytime you stand in line behind some beleaguered-looking person who is buying a new one. Usually, the story ends with some vigorous head-shaking and mumbled sentiments such as "and you know, they'll never catch the bastards."

(I know it is a sexist comment and politically incorrect but the country remains a stubborn bastion of reality-based sentiments. Recent studies have shown that most, if not all, mailbox murderers are adolescent males. There is something about the activity that seems to hold no appeal whatsoever for young women.)

When an evildoer gets caught, there is some satisfaction roundly felt by all who have shared the pain. Any person branded by such a crime would surely have to abandon their neighbourhood or pay a penance so public, the shame would melt his mother's heart.

So it was that a certain courtroom in a certain small town found itself more than half full of onlookers for the first time in anyone's memory.

The accused and a partner had apparently intended to steal a pickup truck from a farmer who they knew always left his keys in the ignition — not at all uncommon behaviour among farmers.

It was a dandy six-month-old, white king-cab, four-wheel-drive baby with four-on-the-floor and raised suspension.

The perpetrators had, in their fashion, thoroughly staked out the area and knew that every Thursday evening, the farmer and his wife attended church choir practice for several hours.

The farm was set back from the road, surrounded by trees, without a clear view of any neighbours.

The plan was for one of the scoundrels to drive the other to the foot of the lane, drop him off and park at the road's edge to watch for any ambient traffic.

Once the stolen truck was at the end of the lane way, the two of them would drive off and do whatever it is one does with a stolen truck.

Ultimately, the issue at trial had little to do with car theft, since the accused pleaded guilty. Stumbling along in the dark, the truck thief had managed to start the truck, but failed to calculate the treachery of the ice that lay under a few inches of fresh snow.

Perhaps nervous, or perhaps just stupid, he had gunned the spunky new truck down the lane with the lights off and ended up doing a doughnut that landed the vehicle squarely in the ditch.

His buddy dutifully drove over and turned on his truck lights to assess the situation. The fellow in the truck turned its lights on, too. Then he tried to gun the truck out of the ditch, and did it with such fervour that the forward thrust sent the truck skidding across the road, where he ran into the mailbox.

The hapless pair were attempting to dislodge the mailbox post from the truck's bumper when a neighbour happened onto the scene. Unfortunately for them, the neighbour also happened to be a cop.

Within the community, knowing the culprits as it did, guilt was presumed. So it came as no surprise that the truck theft charges went unchallenged.

However, to the amazement of all and sundry, when it came to the charge of property damage, the accused firmly responded, "Not guilty, Your Honour."

The prosecution's case seemed open and shut. Not only did they have an eyewitness, they also had Exhibit A, a green metal mailbox, bearing a mortal wound in its left side.

The defendant was representing himself, and the judge invited him to present his case.

"I've done some bad things, some real dumb things," admitted the accused, "but I swear, anything that happened to that mailbox was an accident, pure and simple. I am not the sort of person who whacks mailboxes. I stopped doing that when I turned 20."

In the after-court discussion at the coffee shop, it was generally agreed that the fellow was definitely an inept thief, but arguably not the kind of "so and so" who whacks mailboxes for fun.

The judge levied a fine instead of giving the guy hard time for the mailbox. Everyone agreed that a car thief would probably have an easier time in "The Big House" than somebody up for whacking mailboxes.

In the future, as in the past, victims of "battered mailbox syndrome," or BMS, as the resident experts have designated it, will be forced to live with a faceless enemy intent on destroying a container the size of a breadbox that is empty most of the time.

But even when the road in front of my farm is widened, even when it is paved and painted with a white line, even when the speed limit is raised by rote from 15 kilometres to 125, as appears to be inevitable if drivers' behaviour on the paved crossroads is any indication — making it impossible for anyone in the vehicle to even see a mailbox let alone whack it — I will not subject my old, battered, duct-taped mailbox to even the potential for irreparable harm.

Tucked safely under my arm, the box that has now served me faithfully for a record two and a half years, the fickle box that bears good news as stoically and indifferently as it does bills and flyers will serve its daily purpose and daily be returned to the safe harbour of my front porch.

Even though, from now on, I most certainly will have to look both ways before I cross the road to retrieve it.

THE CAT NOT DEAD

Sometimes when I am out in the garden in the summer time, I find that Webster the Cat is lying under a zucchini leaf or curled up in the middle of the parsley.

"Are you dead yet, Cat?" I ask.

And then slowly, in a remembrance of the languors of youth, he stretches and moves along. The old cat has no new tricks.

And when I say old, I mean it.

Webster is at least eighteen, twice the years that even a nine-lives cat often averages. In cat years to human years ratio terms, he is Methuselah — well over 120.

While he was once a sleek black kitten, Webster is now about as gnarly a cat as anyone has ever seen.

A fine long tail was reduced to a stump years ago by the fan belt of the truck.

His slender ears bear the ragged edges of his years of confrontations with local tomcats and puppies.

His main frame has been buffeted by rams, kicked by cows, tumbled under horses hooves and grazed by everything from Corvettes to manure spreaders.

When he runs, the right side of his body leads and the rest hops after it.

A lump of scar tissue on his belly, where he was once shot clear through by an arrow, has become a sort of talisman that he loves to have rubbed.

When he purrs, his nose scrunches up, revealing fang-like incisors and worn molars. His claws are sharp, but he seldom uses them for defence purposes. When I watch him rolling on his back in the sun on a pile of warm earth, punching his arthritic legs at the clouds like a geriatric prize fighter, I wonder where on earth he gets his stamina.

Stretched flat out like a lizard in the middle of the lane way, Webster looks like a stray piece of wood. But when I call out, "Are you dead yet, Cat?" he creaks to life, if only to turn his head and give me a glimpse of a single crooked fang.

There's not much meat left on those bones, yet Webster's tiny belly is like a bottomless pit.

As a young cat, he lived on dry kibble and an abundance of eggs. If he wanted fresh meat, he caught it himself in the form of barn vermin — mice, rats, the occasional chipmunk, even rabbits.

But dry kibble presents a challenge to Webster's aging choppers. So now, his super-deluxe, getting on in age formula, veterinary marked-up kibble is soaked in homemade chicken and lamb broth. I freeze some stock for him every time I make soup.

He gets meaty table scraps and his eggs are scrambled in milk. He loves turkey dressing and peanut butter cookies.

Webster enjoys feasts that could quell a prison riot, but none of it seems to stick to his ribs. After he eats, his stomach is round, but that's as far as it goes. His bony, cow-hocked back legs have trouble keeping up with his pigeon-toed front legs and he moves like a little old man whose pants are falling down.

Last winter, I thought he was a goner for sure.

In the throes of an ice storm that made walking anywhere a treachery, Webster disappeared for two days. For all I knew, he could have slid down a rabbit hole. Sending out a search party wasn't practical. Moose was away on business, and it was up to me to hold the fort.

The next day, I found Webster curled up on his quilted barn bed, fringed in icicles.

"Are you dead yet, Cat?" I called, fearing the worst.

One scrawny back leg gave a kick and I moved closer to pet him. He lifted his head and I drew my hand back.

Normally, Webster's head is like the size of a mid-season potato, but it had mushroomed to twice its size.

Crested between his ears was a huge boil, an abscess that stretched his skin taut. His amber eyes only half opened and he made a pitiful meow.

It was a Sunday. The roads were closed due to ice. Phone lines were down, hydro often flickered. I set up a heat lamp over Webster and dried him off slowly with the old hair dryer I keep in the barn for use at lambing time. He barely moved.

The storm was in full swing, howling wind and freezing rain. I crawled back to the house on all fours in my snowsuit, it was that slippery. Then I pondered what to do.

Seeing the old cat in so much pain was hardly bearable, but I didn't have it in me to shoot Webster. There had to be another way. I decided to give him an hour to warm up while I formulated a plan.

I knew that if I was similarly afflicted, the doctor would have me on antibiotics. Although I keep injectable antibiotics on the farm for just such extra-ordinary circumstances involving the sheep, there didn't seem enough of Webster left to inject.

In the refrigerator, I found half a dozen antibiotic capsules left over from one of Moose's long-ago toothaches. I scrambled an egg into a tin of tuna and sprinkled a third of a capsule into the mix, topping it with warm milk.

I have always found that if even the sickest animal has the will to eat, there is potential for recovery. My hope was in the Tupperware container that I tucked into my snowsuit for the long crawl back to the barn.

Webster was dry and warm. His favourite rooster had joined him under the heat lamp. I propped the cat up on his elbows and presented "the cure." Sure enough, he lifted his swollen head and lapped up the warm, fishy drug-laced gruel. Then he fell back on the quilt and curled his paws over his face in a deep sleep. Any thought I had about moving him into the house vanished. Webster needed to be in his element, with the smells he knew, and the sounds of the sheep and the storm, and the comfort of his rooster.

I worried that I might have overdosed the cat.

I worried that I might not have given him enough.

Before I went to bed, I crawled out to the barn again, this time through a foot of wet snow. Webster drank his fill of warm medicated milk. Then he dropped back into a deep sleep.

The next morning, the sun shone and the ice-coated landscape sparkled dangerously.

Wally the Wonder Dog shot out the front door. He slid across the lane like a greased medicine ball. When I hunkered down for the ritual barn crawl, Wally tried to hitch a ride on my back and we both splatted on all fours. There is a sense of total unreality that falls over you when both you and your dog are lying on a sheet of ice, looking up at the winter sun.

Wally started licking the chest of my snowsuit. That's when I remembered where I had tucked the Tupperware container with a cat breakfast of beef stew, egg, warm milk and drugs. The crawl back to the house was soggy.

When I finally got into the barn, after reconstituting the cat's food and hacking the ice off the barn door, the sheep shared their greetings. While they *baaed*, I raced to find Webster, hopefully, not dead yet. And he wasn't.

Again he ate heartily. Before he dropped back to sleep, I held his bloated head and stared into his amber eyes. Webster was still in there.

The storm stopped two days later. Early that morning I prepared a list of supplies I needed in town and contemplated calling the vet about Webster.

When I went to the barn, the sheep were bright with anticipation of spending some time outdoors. Webster was gone.

At the back of the shed, I found tiny cat footprints that headed into a field. I imagined him dragging himself out across the snow, like some ancient Eskimo relieving his family of further responsibility.

Then I felt badly because, after all those years, I wanted the responsibility and I felt Webster was cheating me out of seeing him through the final transition.

Well, Webster doesn't disappoint. When I came home from town, he was back under the heat lamp. He jumped to his feet when I came through the door. The lump on his head was substantially gone and he wanted more of my special gruel. Once Webster chowed down, I examined his furry skull and found a festered puncture wound, probably from an encounter with a neighbouring tomcat that had gone badly.

Later, when I held him, bathing the crater in his head and dressing the damaged area, Webbie purred with the vigour of days gone by.

Then he rolled on his quilt, contorting himself into a shape worthy of a yogi.

"You're not dead yet, are you, Cat?" I said, and Webster yawned.

The cat healed nicely. His rooster went back to his roost. In the barnyard, Webster followed me around, picking his way through the snow like a dainty spider.

One of these days, Webster will make transit into the realm of memory. But I wouldn't bet that it will necessarily be any time soon.

In the meantime, if he wants to spend his summer days curled up in the parsley, or underneath the sunflowers where he can watch the blue jays, I say, more power to him.

The amber eye of this barn cat has seen a lot of things, and he's still in there.

THE TOLL GATE CHRISTMAS

Before he even asked them to Christmas supper in July, most people in Northcote already held that Old Jim was crazy.

"Just telling you, is all," Jim would say. "Christmas supper at my place. You're invited. All the trimmings. Gonna grow it all myself."

It was the longest speech that anyone had heard Old Jim give in years.

He lived in a squat stone house at the edge of the village in a small-windowed structure known as "The Toll Gate" because about a hundred and fifty years earlier it had been the residence of the roads dues collector.

Jim kept to himself in the cool darkness of the Toll Gate, and he expected everyone else to mind his privacy. Only the bravest of children ever tried to take a short-cut across Jim's garden to the river.

"Hey, you there," he would shout from behind a cedar thicket. "There's a toll for crossing my land, and I'll have it out of your hide with my musket if you aren't gone by the time I count to ten."

By the time Jim got to "five" the intruders were breathless, past a raspberry patch that marked the property line. No one ever saw the actual musket. Someone heard that a newcomer woman from the subdivision, by the east side of the Northcote, had once knocked on Old Jim's door and told him that he should not be threatening children with firearms. She would report him to the authorities if he ever did it again. Jim swept her off the porch with a broom and told her she'd get hers if she ever set foot on his property again.

To most, he was just a harmless hermit. Picked up his pension cheque as regular as clockwork at the General Store post office. Always paid cash. Took the bus to the farmers' market every other Saturday and brought home whatever he bought in a heavy brown satchel that looked like it had been through the war.

Before Mother Purdie went into the nursing home, she told her son, John Purdie Jr., who everyone just called "Junior," that Jim had been a soldier once. That was why he sometimes dragged his left leg. Shrapnel shifting in his knee. Junior was also told that Jim had even won some medals.

Jim never took a wife. He worked at the feed mill, in the back-shed dust of the granary, until the day his pension kicked in. Then he limped down the hill to the Toll Gate house and slammed the door. A whole generation of villagers grew up after that and not one of them ever saw the inside of the tight, square building where the hermit lived.

Only eight of Northcote's "Old Guard" were invited for Christmas dinner at Old Jim's. Far from feeling snubbed, the rest were relieved.

Christmas in Northcote was always a family affair. People didn't leave Northcote for Christmas, they had relatives and friends come for Christmas. Washed in snow, Northcote was a postcard from Currier & Ives — snug gingerbread houses trimmed with holly and cedar boughs, snowmen in the front yards, toboggans stacked at the side door and skating parties with carollers in the Northcote pavilion.

In the evening, Northcoters retired to home and hearth for their private meal and merriment. They did not abandon ship and crowd into a virtual stranger's house for no apparent reason except an invitation.

In August, a delivery van was spotted in the Toll Gate lane. Katie Purdie, Junior's 11-year-old daughter, peeked through the raspberry bushes and saw Old Jim burning two huge cardboard boxes in his backyard fire pit. The next day, Will, the scrap dealer from Glengate, hauled an ancient Fridgidaire and a two-burner stove off old Jim's front porch.

Amelia Fudger waved at Jim as he lurched toward the General Store to pick up his pension cheque the next Tuesday. Her husband, Tom, had been so surprised when Jim actually talked to him in July that it wasn't until Jim was half a block away that he realized Jim had invited them for Christmas dinner. Amelia had been apoplectic.

Before she had a chance to burble something she had carefully scripted about having to go to the mother-in-law's that Christmas, family illness, could be the last time, grandkids coming from all over, so sorry, maybe next year . . . Jim was looking her square in the face.

"I'll be breaking in the new oven this week," said Jim. "Getting the kinks worked, figuring out the dials and such like. The turkey's at the Welch Farm. Say he's about six pounds now. I give them five dollars a week feed. He'll be 25 pounds by Christmas the way I'm having him grown. Forward to seein' you, Mrs. Fudger."

He was past the picket fence and across the road before Amelia could speak.

"Well, I just wanted to let you know that Tom's mother is sick," she called out.

"Sorry to hear that," said Jim, without turning his head her way.

That evening, Amelia and Tom invited the other six invitees to a Friday-night backyard barbecue to discuss the situation.

On Thursday, Lovett Allen saw Old Jim hauling something in big white pails up from the swamp bush near the river bend. Lovett had barely nodded at Old Jim before he and his wife, Wendy, were invited to the Christmas dinner. Now he was pulling his car over to the roadside to offer Jim a lift.

"Don't bother me none to carry some good black swamp dirt," Jim said, and he just kept walking. "It'll be lighter once I got it cooked anyway. See you in December."

When Lovett Allen shared that tidbit at the Fudger barbecue, the women's necks arched back into their shoulder blades and the men made puffing sounds.

"What in holy hanna's name is he doing cooking swamp dirt?" declared Farrah Carmichael, whose husband, Ned, claimed to have only heard the last half of Old Jim's invitation because he'd had his hearing aid turned way down. Junior was with him at the time, so Ned got the details second-hand. Farrah, his leonine second wife, had been chastising Ned ever since for not putting an end to the invitation right then and there.

"I get you fresh batteries so you can hear and then you don't use them," she sputtered. "Now some crazy old man is cooking us dirt for Christmas dinner."

After considerable delving into Long Island Tea and gin-laced fruit punch, the consensus among the women was that the men were responsible, so the men would have to deal with Old Jim.

Junior's wife, Posey, laid it on the line.

"You got us into this by listening to the old fool in the first place, so you can just get us out of it," Posey said, asserting the full huff of a middle-age-spread that started at her plump ankles and spread all the way to the chins under her chin.

The men stared into their drinks, plucking out imaginary bugs, and pulling on their ears. In the back of their minds each one was thinking the same thing. Christmas was four months away. Plenty of time. Strength in numbers. One of these days.

Labour Day came and went, along with Fall Fair Day and Halloween. Without the summer people passing through the village on their way to the lake, Northcote settled into a hibernation pattern. People trimmed their hedges for the last time, mulched their gardens with burnished maple leaves and checked their roofs for loose shingles.

Every Friday night, Farrah and Ned fought. It was a one-sided sort of affair. Farrah spat words at Ned, and he nodded in her general direction, careful to turn his "good ear" away from her volley. It was a trick he used all the time when salespeople tried to talk him into something at the hardware store he had managed for years.

Farrah wasn't just on about the Christmas dinner. She scattered her thoughts like a shotgun pattern. It was the usual second-wife stuff and nonsense. She wanted to redecorate the bedroom. She wanted different towels. She wanted her own pots and pans. She needed to feel the house was her space, and on and on. If only *he* didn't have to make alimony payments, *they* could have a life, but what kind of a life was it when they couldn't even sit down together for a private Christmas dinner?

The other men suffered as well, to varying degrees. Tom Fudger was just two bites into his Thanksgiving pumpkin pie when Amelia announced that he had already "spoiled Christmas."

The fact was that Tom's ailing mother had moved to California to live with his sister and her family. Too far to travel — Amelia worried that the separation might give the cats fur-ball attacks. The only Fudger child, Gordon, sent a letter in October saying that he planned to go skiing in Vermont with his university pals over Christmas. Since Amelia had come to what she termed "odds" with her side of the family, the Fudgers would be alone in Northcote for the holidays.

"I don't know about you, but I plan on having some virulent, contagious disease for Christmas," wailed Amelia. "And if you're just lucky, I'll give it to you, so we don't have to go to some stupid place where we don't belong, to sit with a bunch of spineless wimps and eat gawd knows what cooked by a psychopath."

Wendy and Lovett Allen were also considering disease options.

"We could say you've got the gout and I have to tend you," Wendy offered brightly.

But Lovett was organizing the Christmas Day skating party and Wendy was the only soprano of the carollers. They considered themselves indispensable to the community.

"Well, you'll just have to sprain your ankle or something when its over," Wendy said. "I don't mean really, mind, just a pretend thing, so we can make our excuses and be done with the whole thing."

Posey and Junior had another problem. Early on, it was apparent to Posey that the men were a leader-less group, lacking in imagination and destined to fumble their way to Christmas dinner at the Toll Gate regardless of their instructions. Junior had even started saying aloud that it might be kind of interesting to have a look inside the Toll Gate house. They would be having Christmas lunch after church with his mother at the nursing home, so there was no need to do more than nibble whatever it was Old Jim planned to serve. Could be interesting, something different and for just a few hours.

"And what do you think we're supposed to do with Katie?" an exasperated Posey asked, after one of Junior's more elaborate rambles. "It's her Christmas, too. Am I supposed to throw a turkey TV dinner in the oven for her and leave her alone on Christmas night? Have you lost your senses?" Perhaps he had, Junior thought benignly. Christmas was already taking its toll.

A few days after the first snowfall in November, Posey picked Katie up from school and drove over to the Toll Gate. They walked up to the front door, Posey more purposefully than Katie, who clutched her back-pack full of school books in front of her in case they were met by a musket.

Jim answered on the third knock. He didn't seem surprised to see them.

"Oh yes, Mrs. Purdie it is and you, you're that young one in the raspberry bushes I see now and then," he said, giving a wink at Katie that Posey judged wholly inappropriate.

"Well, that's just it, Jim," started Posey. "The Christmas dinner and all, well Junior and I just wouldn't feel right leaving Katie alone and I know how you feel about children, so I guess we just can't make it."

Jim didn't move to speak.

"Well, maybe you could come over to our place on Boxing Day for brunch or something and tell us all about it," Posey spouted. "Or another time, you know, New Year's or something."

She began backing away from the porch.

"Oh now, Mrs. Purdie, I didn't mean for you to take it wrong. Of course, Katie's invited, too. I mean the turkey's already 24 pounds and there's weeks of growing left to do," he said.

Posey's face scrunched involuntarily and Katie swished her lips from side to side, the way she always did when something wasn't quite going as planned.

"And I've an idea to go with that," Jim said, running his hand up over his smooth-shaven chin. "I could use a helper getting things ready. Of course, I'd pay you Katie and it wouldn't take much of your time. Help you get something a little extra for Christmas and you'd be helping out an old man. No muskets, I promise."

Katie Purdie was a willful girl. She had flecks of gold in her hazel eyes that her grandmother said meant she was destined for riches and glory.

"It'll be $6.35 an hour, that's minimum wage," said Katie. "And double if I have to do anything on Christmas Day."

"Done," said Jim, "Come over Saturday at noon and we'll figure some things out." He held out his hand to seal the deal.

Posey carried Katie's backpack to the car. She was so mad she could feel her feet swelling inside her fur-trimmed boots.

Katie knew better than to smile or even say a word. She didn't have to. Imagine being paid to get first-hand information about the Northcote Hermit and the Tortures of Toll Gate. Everyone would want to know. If there was a dungeon — and everyone knew that there must be a dungeon — she could draw pictures of it and sell them right from the back of the school bus.

Old Jim didn't scare Katie. He was right, she had watched him from the raspberry bushes and all she saw was an old man working in his garden, listening to old-time music and feeding the birds. Big deal, so he needed his windows cleaned or whatever, she had to do that at home for free.

Posey was poised when Junior got home that evening. It started with, "Now you won't believe what your daughter has gotten us into," and it went on from there. The last thing Katie heard before she fell asleep was Posey wailing: "Anthrax is too good for us. We are cursed."

Winter

Every passing day brought the Northcote Eight 24 hours closer to Christmas. Life went on. Christmas lights went up on the gingerbread. Flannelette sheets went down on the beds. The Santa Claus parade rolled through without a hitch, and pots of poinsettias could be viewed through most front windows. No one would have guessed that in four separate houses, plans were being made, casting a pox on Christmas.

Katie was tight-lipped about the goings on at Toll Gate, although she made no secret of her growing bank account. She told her parents Jim just had her doing "stuff," like cleaning the windows and beating some old rugs. It wasn't awful. Still, her mother noticed that Katie came home with dirty fingernails. The place must be a pig sty.

"What's mileage?" Katie asked her mother, when she came home after the second of her four-hour-long Saturday sessions at Toll Gate. "I don't mean like, how many miles are on the car, I mean what's it worth like to move something around?"

"Why, is he planning on kidnapping you?" Posey asked. Katie was taking Old Jim all too seriously from her perspective. Mileage, indeed.

"Well, he wants me to have some stuff dry-cleaned and gave me the money, but said he'd pay mileage, too, because I have to get you to drive it to the cleaners."

Then Katie hauled a lace tablecloth out of a garbage bag she dragged home across the snow. It was a filigree of fancy handiwork the colour of pale tea.

"This goes underneath," said Kate, pulling out a fine linen cloth that was sturdy, but yellowed at the edges where it had been carefully folded. A swath of napkins followed.

Posey called Farrah Carmichael for an opinion.

"These are serious antiques," Farrah said, with the authority of a woman who can tell the difference between 200 and 220 thread count in a bed sheet with just one touch.

"The linen is definitely Irish, but the lace-work has Bruges written all over it." Although she had never been to the lace capital of Belgium, Farrah prided herself on her pronunciation, squeezing out "Bruges" precisely as though ready to rhyme it with "ooze."

"I would set this with my Polish crystal and the Rosenthal china," said Farrah, fingering the napkins. "But never mind that. We've decided that Ned is going to get an earache in his good ear. That way, I have to stay home with him, because when his good ear goes wonky it makes him dizzy just trying to stand up. Good, eh."

The Fudgers were rumoured to have laid groundwork for a quiet sort of disease, one that would strike suddenly, but disappear for their annual New Year's Eve party. Farrah found out about this in the Town & Country ladieswear store, where she had spotted Amelia trying on a hot pink down-lined ski suit.

"Now you know she doesn't ski," said Farrah. "She always says she's too brittle to do almost everything.

So I asked her what she was doing and she said the suit was her protection for when she swoons after the Christmas skating party and Tom has to take her home with a sudden syndrome of some sort."

"At this stage, I'd settle for haemorrhoids," Posey said glumly. "For Junior, of course, not myself. Except I don't know if a horse's ass can get haemorrhoids. He actually asked me last week if I thought we should take some wine over to Jim's Christmas dinner! Then Katie pops her head up and says, 'It's all taken care of.'"

"Well, at least you'll be eating whatever you're eating off a clean tablecloth," said Farrah, caressing the lace-work."Odd, the whole thing is odd."

By the first week of December, the ice had frozen on Northcote Pond. Snow fell in beautiful crystalline blankets, curling across close-cropped lawns and hedge tops.

Wendy Allen and Amelia Fudger ran into Don Welch at the farmers' market on a Saturday morning in the middle of the month. The place was alive with the scent of cedar boughs and cinnamon. Tinny strains from familiar Christmas songs blended with the boot-steps of people bobbing and jostling through the red-bowed aisles filled with crafts and baked goods.

"Old Jim's turkey is a monster bird, at least 28 pounds, I told him today," Don Welch called out from behind the deli counter, where the Welch Farm's free-range turkeys lay in vacuum-sealed rows in front of the smoked turkey parts and the turkey salami. "We're plucking him on the 23rd. You ladies are in for a treat."

Wendy and Amelia nodded in his direction, smiling as they hurried away. In the parking lot they patted the shoulders of their winter parkas as though something dirty had brushed them. Neither of them had revealed their plans to escape from attending the Toll Gate supper to the other, but now they were both committed to the idea.

Their husbands were professionals. Wendy had helped put Lovett Allen through law school by teaching piano lessons from their cramped off-campus apartment. Tom Fudger, a chartered accountant, had plucked Amelia out of the steno pool and made her his wife, much to the dismay of his mother who always thought he could have done better.

"Isn't there some law against telling everyone your business?" Wendy demanded of Lovett, as soon as he came home. "I can't even go shopping without everyone knowing that my Christmas supper is some sort of custom-killed monster ordered up by a geezer who looks like Ichabod Crane."

Lovett gazed out the bay window, sucking on his pipe, watching the snow fall.

"I don't think there's any case law, honey," he said.

Amelia Fudger sulked. She had a terrible feeling that even if she keeled over dead in her pink ski suit at the skating party, somebody would plant her at the Toll Gate table and shove a fork in her hand. As was his custom, Tom steered clear of his wife when she was in one of her moods. He had actually seen Jim outside the farmers' market on his way home. Offered the old boy a ride, but he wouldn't take it.

"Got another stop to make," Jim said. The brown satchel looked fairly heavy to Tom, but he didn't ask any questions.

Two days before Christmas, Katie Purdie announced that she had never seen a turkey that big before. She had stopped at Toll Gate house on her way home from school and she was there when Don Welch delivered the bird.

"Jim's oven is bigger'n ours," she told her mother.

Posey snorted at this piece of trivia, but Junior found it comforting.

"At least there will be enough dark meat to go around," he said.

"Salmonella, you mean," Posey muttered. She would not be touching turkey on Christmas Day, no matter what. Farrah Carmichael had already pre-cooked two Cornish Game Hens that she could just pop in the microwave. Even Old Mother had told Junior that they didn't have to stay after church and lunch with her at the nursing home because the turkey there was bound to be too dry to swallow.

Of course, the twenty-fifth day of December arrived. Presents were opened and hymns were sung.

Northcote glistened in the winter sun like a polished ornament. Around two in the afternoon people began filtering into the street, waving their new gloves at each other as they walked down the snow-covered road to the skating pond.

The carollers were already under the gazebo sorting out song sheets. Lovett Allen had been down earlier to check the ice, and gave it a final going-over with the blade attached to his lawn tractor. Then he decided to put the ice to the test. Wendy watched him lace up his skates while she blew her pitch pipe, sounding the highest note she would have to reach in "Hark the Herald Angels Sing."

The Fudgers and the Carmichaels walked down together. Ned wore a new pair of ear muffs, but he knew from watching Farrah's wide mouth and flashing white teeth that she was explaining the provenance of the new pots and pans he had given her. He reached in his pocket and savoured the warmth of the finely etched silver flask full of brandy that she had given him.

"A little something to help you with your wonky ear routine, my darling," Farrah told him, when he unwrapped it. Then she rubbed Ned's cheeks with one of her bath towels and purred something about the joys of Egyptian cotton.

While Farrah was fairly prancing down the road, Amelia Fudger clung to Tom's hand, afraid that she would slip and fall before she had a chance to swoon.

Her face was already as pink as her ski suit. Tom wished they had taken the car.

The pond was covered with skaters by the time the Purdies arrived.

Both Posey and Junior were surprised that Katie had allowed herself a special moment with her grandmother before leaving the nursing home. With her own money, Katie had bought her a blue cashmere shawl.

"You look cool, Gran," she said, wrapping the new shawl around Mother Purdie.

But once they got home, prying Katie away from her new computer games had not been easy. When she finally got her skates on, the sun was dodging clouds and the carollers were breathing stiffly as the temperature dropped.

Wendy Allen couldn't hit high C under the circumstances. After two hours, the Northcote singers decided to call it quits

When Lovett saw his wife leaving the gazebo, he knew it was time. When he was almost certain no one was watching him, he skated in a zig-zag and made a sharp right turn. Letting his skates slip out from under, he slid gently to the ice and sat there. Then he reached for his ankle and continued sitting there. Finally, his wife came skidding across the ice to his side. And a few people had noticed he was no longer skating.

Amelia Fudger swooned at exactly four o'clock. There wasn't much of a sound, she was just standing on a snow bank near the footbridge one minute and lying on the ice the next. Tom had gone to get hot chocolate and missed the whole thing when he got caught up in a discussion about tax rebates.

The pond was divided into two crowds. In the centre of the ice, Lovett Allen hunched over his right foot, emitting sporadic groans he hoped sounded convincing. Wendy wrung her hands and worried aloud about how to move him. Had Lovett only decided to fake a broken collar bone he could have at least walked home. He didn't even have enough sense to fall close to the pathway.

"How about the tractor?" said Katie.

Lovett agreed that if someone could drive the lawn tractor to him he could probably manage to drive himself off the ice. Wendy took off his skates and tried wrapping his foot with her new plaid scarf, until Laura Douglas, the school nurse, insisted that packing the injured ankle in snow was the correct procedure. Lovett howled for real, while Katie skated off to find Ned Carmichael who had sold the Allens the tractor in the first place.

At the base of the footbridge snow bank, Amelia lay perfectly still. If she got lucky, her ski suit might be in pristine enough condition for her to return it when this was all over. If not, she thought that she probably looked pretty good, with colour-coordinated lipstick and South Sea Mabe pearl earings.

Someone picked up her wrist and took her pulse with an icy finger. Amelia now stayed still as a pink popsicle. Yes, she was alive. Now where was that husband of hers?

A long minute passed. When Tom finally knelt beside her she could smell hot chocolate when he cupped his hands to her face. Amelia's left eyelid fluttered, but the mascara on her right eye had frozen to her lower lid.

It's one of her swoons, happens now and then," Tom explained, calmly.

"See, no blood."

He started to lift Amelia's head as proof but voices from the crowd were adamant that she not be moved. No one had seen her fall, there was just a large gouge in the snow bank. Cell phones flipped open like shucked oysters and protective arms pulled Tom away.

"She just swoons and that's usually it," he said pathetically. Amelia heard words like "coma" and "concussion" bandied about.

Katie found Ned and Farrah Carmichael with her parents on the far side of the pond. They hadn't noticed the goings on, but Ned was slumped against Junior's shoulder.

"First really cold weather and his good ear always goes wonky," Farrah kept saying to passers-by. "Makes him lose his balance. Poor baby can hardly stand." Then she took off Ned's ear muffs. "Look, he can't even hear a thing now."

Posey Purdie had heard it all before, but had no idea that Ned could mimic the condition so convincingly.

"Mr. Allen's broken his foot or something and we've got to get Mr. Carmichael to take the tractor out and get him," said Katie. She was so concerned that she skated right into her mother, pushing Posey close enough to Ned for her to catch a strong scent of brandy.

Ned straightened right up.

"What, Lovett's hurt? Where? Get me the keys," he shouted. "I'm on the way, Lovett, hang in there." Then he waved his arms at the crowd, flung himself away from Junior and wobbled off in the general direction of the lawn tractor.

A pair of ear muffs were airborne across the ice. Posey shrugged at Farrah. Junior felt them whiz past his shoulder but he was focussed on the crowd gathering at the foot bridge.

"What's going on?" he asked the postmistress, who was already heading home.

"Didn't you know? Amelia Fudger's got a coma or something from falling off the snow bank," she said. "Poor Tom says it happens all the time."

"Oh my gosh," said Katie, skating away, while her father trailed, shuffling across the ice in rubber boots.

Katie had a full news report before her father reached the halfway point.

"She's just lying there all pink and everything with her eyes closed," she told Junior. "And Mr. Fudger says it's not a coma, but it's something else and it's happened before. No one knows why she fell, or if she got pushed."

Junior saw the school nurse in the crowd around Lovett and he headed in that direction. Lovett was sitting upright on the ice with his Wendy's scarf packed full of snow wrapped around his ankle. Someone had stuck a blue mitten over his toes to keep them from freezing.

"Is it bad?" Junior asked Wendy, who had stayed at his side throughout the ordeal.

"Sprained, we think," she said, wishing to high heaven that Lovett had only gone down closer to the road. They could have been home having hot toddies on the sofa by now.

"You'll be all right, Ned's warming the tractor up now to come and get you," Junior said, leaning into Lovett's ear. "Anyway, there should be an ambulance coming to get Amelia if you need one."

"A what?" cried Lovett.

"An ambulance. I mean she's that out of it, lying over by the footbridge," Junior said. "She's not in a coma, which is good, but nobody knows if she was pushed or she fell. I'm going to have the nurse take a look at her. Okay."

If there was one thing that Lovett Allen could see coming as clearly as a train down a track, it was litigation. The wooden footbridge had needed repairs in the fall, but nobody had gotten around to it. Northcote could be held responsible. Or what if it was a crime scene and people were tramping all over the evidence?

"Gotta get there," he said, grabbing Junior firmly by his knee and reaching out for his hand. His right foot was supposedly sprained, but it was his left foot that gave him the most trouble because it had fallen asleep.

"What do you think you're doing?" Nurse Douglas demanded, as Lovett clung to Junior's shoulders, his right foot firmly planted on the ice and left foot jerking in spasms of pins and needles.

"Call it a miracle. Feels fine now," Lovett called, as he hopped along the ice, braced against Junior, with Wendy following behind, holding his skates and chasing after her scarf as it slowly unwound. By the time Ned caught up to them on the tractor, Lovett was striding forcefully in his wet socks.

Feeling distinctly chilly on the ice, Amelia Fudger hadn't figured on anyone calling an ambulance, but she couldn't just jump to her feet and call it off. She decided to give her head a shake to attract Tom's attention, but he was standing on top of the footbridge looking for lights and listening for sirens.

Instead, the first people to recognize signs of life in Amelia were Farrah and Posey, who had decided they just had to catch Amelia's act.

"She moved, did you see that," Posey noted.

Farrah kneeled beside the body, so close that her long blond hair grazed Amelia's face.

"Come out, come out, wherever you are," Farrah sang, and Amelia's eyes fluttered open.

After being prone for such a long time, Amelia was actually a bit woozy as Farrah and Posey helped her to her feet. The pinkness drained from her cheeks, and she reached out for Tom, who had, seeing her helped up, slid down the snow bank as easily as she had. As they embraced, the chilled hot chocolate Tom was still carrying splashed across the front of the pink ski suit.

"Watch it," Amelia said, jumping back smartly, twisting her shoulders and regaining her posture.

"You're all right, thank god," croaked Lovett Allen, sliding to a stop and wrapping his arms around them. Hopping from one foot to the other, he grabbed the nearest cell phone and cancelled the ambulance which had yet to arrive.

On the west side of the pond, Ned ran the tractor into a clump of ice. It was still running when Farrah pulled him off.

"I don't wanna hear. I don't wanna hear," he kept saying, while her steady torrent of derision drove him toward the footbridge.

In the near dark of the late afternoon, Katie took her skates off. Most of Northcote had already returned to their hearths. Wood-burning smells filled the air and the word was picking up.

"It's almost time for supper, so I'm going straight to the Toll Gate," Katie said. "See you all in an hour."

Posey Purdie had always known it would come to this. Now the others knew it, too. Amelia wanted a nice hot bath. Farrah wanted to shove Ned in a cold shower. Wendy found Lovett's shoes in a corner of the gazebo, and they all started up the hill.

"You sure don't have to skate to have a good time in this town, do you," Junior said. No one responded.

At seven p.m. the doors of four houses reluctantly opened and closed. While they traditionally dressed up for Christmas supper, this time the women didn't bother. Farrah was the only one bearing a gift.

"Chocolates," she sniffed. "Left over from last year's staff party. I hope."

A plain grapevine wreath decorated the Toll Gate house door. Old Jim had made it himself from the wild vines that grew in a tangle on his cedar rail fence. Katie took their coats, while boots were stacked on a raised board to dry in the narrow entrance way.

Wearing a green wool vest with leather buttons over his usual red flannel shirt, Jim shook their chilled hands one by one as they moved into the main room. It was gridded by thick wooden beams that separated it from the dining room and pantry, which were raised a few steps higher.

"Figure you might want to warm those toes up, Mr. Allen," Old Jim said, guiding the barrister to a well-padded Morris chair beside the fireplace. The planked pine wood floor bore the scars of cinders past. On the other side of the room, there were scattered braided rugs that overlapped each other around a long dining table only partially revealed.

"Lovett, call me Lovett," insisted the weary barrister, who, like everyone else, was still trying to get his bearings. The light was soft, cast from tassel-trimmed spindle lamps and a pair of copper and brass sconces that hung beside a roll-top desk in the front corner.

The Toll Gate house smelled the way Christmases were supposed to smell. There was something of turkey and turnips, mixed with baking buns and boiling potatoes and lemon oil. Posey Purdie picked up the distinct scent of lemon oil from the wainscotting.

She lowered herself carefully into a corner seat on the earth-brown sofa and ran her hand along a log-cabin quilt stitched in kaleidoscope colours before finally settling in.

"It won't bite," Jim said. "How about some grog?"

"Grog" turned out to be hot tea with a hint of honey and a larger hint of rum. A thin brown cinnamon stir stick stood out of the lip of each mug. Ned smiled and turned his good ear to the crackle of the cherry logs in the stone fireplace, while Farrah shoved her chocolate box on the end pine table, where she thought it might blend in with the stack of *National Geographics*.

Conversation picked up when Jim called out from the kitchen that he had seen some of the commotion on the pond, but Katie had told him that it looked worse than it was.

Amelia started on about how she still felt woozy and Tom gave her a warning look. Posey's chin slipped into her other chin disapprovingly.

"Can't do too much damage at a skating party," Junior piped up. "You ever been to one, Jim?"

"He watches," answered Katie, hopping up the steps and heading for the kitchen as though she owned the place.

"Seen 'em all, only got close once," Jim said, coming into view beside the largest beam, where he wiped his hands on a woman's half apron decorated with candy canes Wendy Lovett recognized it from one of the stalls at the farmers' market.

"One I remember best, most of you wouldn't because you came on later. It was when young Purdie fell through the ice and they had to use a hockey stick to pull him out," Jim said, feeling Posey's eyes intent on him. "Remember that Junior? I helped your mother carry you home, never saw her so worried then or since. Now that was excitement."

Junior was speechless. Crazy old Jim was going on about his private shame, in front of everyone.

"So that's why you never skate," said Farrah. "Ned can't skate because of the ear-balance thing, but if I ever fell through ice I would never go near it again."

Junior's only memory of that day was the paralyzing terror and holding his breath even after he came up for air. He had never thought about how he got home that day, but even as a young woman, Mother Emma Purdie could never have carried a half-frozen seven-year-old up the Northcote hill by herself.

"I guess I owe you a big debt of gratitude," Junior said, toasting Jim with a mug of steaming grog that Katie had refilled.

"Thank your mother, she's the one who called me out to help. She should be here soon, anyway."

Jim went back to the kitchen and there was a clatter of pans. Lovett looked at Junior and Posey shrugged for both of them . . . as though they had a collective mind, the women all rose at the same time to see if they could help in the kitchen.

Katie was putting the dessert forks at the top of each place setting when the women stormed the doorway to the kitchen. Farrah Carmichael had to catch her breath. The table was set with Polish crystal and Rosenthal china, not her pattern but if she thought for a moment she was sure she could name it.

"Nice, eh," said Katie. "Jim had it shipped home for his mother after the war. Only two teacups broke."

"What a lovely tablecloth," Farrah called out. "Belgian lace, is it?"

"Don't know about that," Jim said, running a basting brush over the nut-brown turkey he had pulled from the oven for the others to inspect. "It was a gift from some Dutch people I met when we liberated one of those Holland towns."

Farrah had a lot of questions about the silver candlesticks on the table, but before she could ask them there was a knock at the door. It was Don Welch dropping off Mother Purdie.

Jim went to greet them and he invited Don to share a cup of grog.

"Can't," he said, "big snow coming and I'm wanted at home. But I do want to see the bird." Brushing his boots off, Don walked through the crowd to the kitchen, nodding as he went.

Amelia and Wendy stood back to give the turkey grower a good view.

"Yessir, when it comes to growing a turkey, I'm a real pro. Ya done good on him, Jim." Then he left as smoothly as he entered.

Mother Purdie had dressed for Christmas supper. Wrapped over her cranberry wool dress she wore the blue shawl. Junior offered his mother his seat on the sofa and she settled back comfortably.

"Just tea for me is fine," she told Katie. "The grog is my old recipe, but I think I'm just too old for that now."

There was an air of discomfort in the Toll Gate house. In the kitchen, the women marvelled at the level of organization — the carving set honed and ready, gravy boats lined up, buns in the warming oven with the vegetables and potatoes draining over the sink, ready to be mashed.

"Is it time to pick the salad yet?" Katie asked.

"You do it," said Jim. "I've got mashing to tend to."

"Two at a time if you want to see," Katie told the room. "It's growing in the basement and things are kind of crowded down there."

"This must be the swamp-dirt part," Farrah said.

Lovett Allen was first in line.

"He couldn't use dirt, too much disease," Katie explained, opening a door that stood near the fireplace beside one of the small square windows that looked out over the snow-covered garden.

"It's all grown hydroponically. Careful, Mr. Allen, the ceiling's kind of low as people were shorter in the old days."

In the middle of the room above a floor that was definitely dirt, a system of white fluorescent lights was suspended over a table covered with greenery.

"I planted the red leaf lettuce, and we already had one harvest," said Katie, pulling tender leaves one by one from one of the trays. "We have three kinds of lettuce, and parsley and the usual stuff. The cucumbers take a lot of space, so there are only two plants."

People were still moving up and down the stairs long after Katie completed her harvest and returned with a colander filled with young greens.

"Let me see," said Mother Purdie. "Old Jim said he'd do it and I guess he did, just like in the magazine."

"You knew about this?" asked Posey with amazement.

"Oh yes, Jim's been talking about growing a winter supper for a long time. Just didn't want me to tell you about it until he had it all figured out."

"Then you two see each other?" Her daughter-in-law's eyes were as wide as saucers.

"He comes every Saturday, just like you, only later in the day," Mother Purdie replied matter-of-factly, scooting Katie off to the kitchen.

When dinner was called, everyone took their places at the name cards that Jim had whittled into business-card-sized slivers of wood and coloured with ink.

"He's a bloody old man Martha Stewart," Farrah said, under her breath. She was seated at the far end of the table, on Ned's good ear side, but Jim heard her.

"Oh, Martha doesn't know everything," he said. *"The Joy of Cooking* has been like a Bible to me, one of the old editions that they have in the library. That and Emma, here." Jim nodded toward Mother Purdie.

Posey Purdie was busting to know what those two had in common and why she was even at the table. Her neck twitched when she got like that and she looked a bit like a chunky, restless chicken. Junior knew the signs.

"So what's this all about, Jim," he said, when the separate platters piled with white and dark meat finally arrived.

"Not yet. First say Grace," said Jim, and heads were bowed while he said something about fine food and fine women and Christmas. Katie poured the wine. Lovett Allen sniffed, sipped and nodded his approval.

Buns passed. Jim baked them himself. He hadn't grown the wheat but after all those years at the mill, he knew what good flour was when he saw it. The yams and potatoes had been harvested from his garden, as had the turnips and carrots.

Posey Purdie liked the carrots, until she saw some small, dark oblong flecks in the orange. She almost dropped her fork, thinking they might be mouse droppings.

"Caraway seeds," said Jim, reading her mood. "You harvest them, dry them and roast them a bit. Most herbs, you want the young leaves, but I like the caraway seeds."

The meal was a marvel to all concerned. Mrs. Purdie said it was the best turkey she'd ever eaten, and the biggest she'd ever seen in a roast pan. Jim glowed.

"And I'm afraid it's my last turkey at the Toll Gate," he said with a sigh, while the women removed the plates.

Before the salad was served (quite properly *after* the main course, as Farrah Carmichael observed), Jim put an old Edith Piaf record on what was probably the last turntable in existence in Northcote.

"Not Christmassy, tired of that stuff," he said. With candles it was perfect.

"See, I'm moving," said Jim, "and that's why I wanted you all here. To tell you and to give you all something.

"I'm old as dirt and I can't run the place the way I used to. So I'm goin' to the nursing home. Got the room next to Emma's reserved." He nodded again toward Mother Purdie. She smiled and Junior took note.

"Thing is the Toll Gate house is history. You folks all live in old houses in town, so you know what I mean. The Toll Gate is the second-oldest building in Northcote, after the front part of the church.

"So what I propose is to give the Toll Gate house to Northcote. Lock, stock, and barrel. Get Lovett to draw up the paper work, Tom to handle the books and Ned to organize whatever fixing-up needs to be done to make it whatever you want. I figure the women can sort that out because they've got the sense for that sort of thing."

Then he left the table and retrieved a square metal box from underneath the sideboard, sliding it across the floor on a scatter rug and hoisting it to the table.

"Found this inside the old cistern down near the raspberry patch, must have been 20 years ago. It's the old toll box, and it's chock full of coins. Mother always told me it was around the house somewhere. Should have gone to the town a long time ago, but my father's father hid it for safe-keeping during one of those rebellions they used to have, and then he got himself shot.

"With a musket, right?" said Katie.

"That's what I was told," smiled Jim.

He opened the latches on the box and turned the contents toward the table. Coins rattled forward, odd-sized and tarnished grey.

"They're not much to look at now, but I sent a handful to a coin specialist and they clean up nice."

Jim pulled a small wad of plastic-covered coins from the pocket of his vest.

"These five here came back with a value of about $1,000 for the lot. Different prices for each one and all kinds of reasons, including how many curls you can count on Queen Victoria's head.

"I don't know what the whole lot of them is worth, but it should be enough to pay the taxes for a few years and give the thing a start.

"All I ask is that I can putter around in the garden. Don't matter to me if the kids cut across anymore. Just so long as it stays and doesn't become some sort of stacked-up subdivision. So that's the thing of it, why I wanted you here. Jim paused and looked at Mother Purdie. "If it's all right with Junior and his Missus, Mother Purdie and me are fixing to get married in the Spring. Miss Katie's already agreed to help me grow the supper, for that one too."

Jim sat down and patted Emma's hand.

Dessert was a huge trifle served from a cut-glass bowl. Old coins passed from hand to hand. Lovett and Tom were talking about trusts. Jim brought out a bottle of brandy that he said was half as old as dirt. Ned wandered around knocking on the old wooden beams. By the fireplace, three generations of Purdies poured over a scrapbook of newspaper clippings Jim had kept ever since the war. Posey orchestrated the clean-up crew in the kitchen, where the women were already arguing about the historic site versus day-care centre.

When they left the Toll Gate house that night, the Northcote Eight, and even Katie, were slow walking up the hill.

"And all this time, I thought old Jim was crazy," Junior allowed pensively, between puffs on his pipe. Posey Purdie just shook her head and stamped her feet. No one else said a word.

WHEN SLEIGH BELLS RING

In rural communities, if a town is large enough to have a Main Street, you can bet that it has a Santa Claus parade. This tradition usually involves giant transport trailer trucks, fire engines, police cars with intrusive siren and tractors trimmed with Christmas lights. Drum majorettes strut and men in skirts play Christmas carols on sheep bladders. The grand finale is St. Nick himself, and the whole thing ends in a rage of shopping that warms the hearts of the members of the local Chamber of Commerce.

But in one southwestern Ontario village, there is a distinctly different parade. No lights, no sirens, no fossil fuel fumes, no commercials, and nowhere much to shop afterward.

Instead, Holstein, Ontario, 100 km north-west of Toronto, hosts a non-mechanized Santa Claus parade featuring the clip clop of homemade, horse-drawn floats and cutters, and the vocal charms of local choirs. There are no razzle-dazzle bands, but a gaggle of children plays "Joy to the World" and other seasonal favourites on multi-coloured plastic kazoos.

The whole parade lasts less than an hour. At the end, free hot dogs are served at the pavilion in the village park where a child-oriented Snofest features such activities as wreath tossing and photo sessions with Santa.

When sleigh bells ring in Holstein everybody listens. Six years ago, when the first old-fashioned Christmas parade marched down the road past the Holstein General Store and the Feed Mill, it was primarily local people who clawed their way through a December fog to watch the horses go by and wave to friends who festooned pony carts and hay wagons with homemade nativity scenes and garland-wrapped trees.

But word has spread about this environmentally friendly homespun parade. For the past couple of Christmases, several thousand visitors have lined the 1.5 km parade route. And for many urbanites who come from Kitchener, Guelph, Collingwood and, yes, even Toronto, it is quite overwhelming.

It is not uncommon to see tears well up in middle-aged eyes.

Last year's parade featured nearly 50 animal-powered entries, including two teams of miniature horses, one donkey, two cows and an unidentified number of dogs wearing reindeer ears.

There is nothing overtly pretentious about the parade — cedar bows on wagons are often affixed with duct tape — but the sentiment is sincere, genuine and infectious.

"People pass each other on the sidewalk saying 'Merry Christmas,' and everybody is smiling or singing," marvelled University of Guelph professor Nancy Ellwand.

A second-time visitor, Ellwand's three children were so captivated that they wanted to be a part of the parade. Kazoo Band organizer Dinah Christie happily accommodated their mother's request.

"There's a lot of leeway in this parade," says actor/ singer Christie, who has a farm nestled in the rolling hills surrounding the village. "Besides, you don't have to know much about music to play the kazoo — as Bacall said to Bogart: 'You just put your lips together and blow.'"

Seventy-year-old Lyle Rawn has been in the parade from the beginning with his grey Percherons, Bud and Duke. He prepares the horses by taking them for long sleigh rides across the fields of the family farm on the outskirts of the village.

The day before the parade, he brings "the boys" into his heated shed and washes their white manes and tails until they gleam.

"I don't have fancy show harnesses, but I like them to look good," says Rawn, who is by no means the oldest driver in the parade. His 76-year-old cousin, Russell, brings a team of chestnut and cream Belgian horses.

The hooves of the big draft horses are the size of pie plates, and they clomp along the snow-covered route guided by seasoned drivers who like nothing better than to show off their gentle giants. There is even an eight-horse mounted choir, whose songs are interspersed with the occasional whinny.

While it looks simple, assembling a non-mechanized parade has its own peculiar problems and rules. Although Holstein is home to Baxter, a fifteen-year-old Bactrium camel owned by the area's Member of Parliament Murray Calder, Baxter is banned from the parade.

"Horses go wild at the smell and sight of a camel," explains Parade Marshall Dennis Boychuk.

Starting in the spring, Boychuk begins making casual rounds of interested parade participants, checking out training programs, harnesses and "overall character."

By parade day, he knows every driver and every horse by name from Linda Raeburn's shaggy Shetland pony Dazzle to Allan Horsburgh's prize-winning grey and black Percherons, Dick and Jed. In between there are elegant Arabians, high-stepping Morgan horses and unknown quantities such as Squiggly, a nine-month-old, sleigh-pulling calf.

"Once we even had a lady walking a lamb," laughs Boychuk, who sets the order of the parade according to the temperament of the animals and their handlers' skill. Santa's sleigh always comes last, pulled by a reliable team of bays named Bob and Reuben.

The whole extravaganza costs less than $1,500 to produce, with horse owners providing their fancy-dressed rigs at their own expense and the local Boy Scouts stuffing goody bags for the kids.

"Everyone pitches in and it seems to bring out the best in people," admits organizer Erika Matheson, who taps volunteer resources from nearly all of the 117 families in the village.

"It's special all right," confides Lyle Rawn. "And you know why? I think it's because the horses like the parade as much as the people."

NO AULD LANG SYNE

So far, after two decades on the farm, excepting matters of life and death, taking down the Christmas tree is the hardest thing I do every year. This follows with some logic, since putting the tree up is one of the hardest things I do at the end of each year.

I'm not saying that this year's tree was necessarily any larger or complex than in any other years. All of the trees that have graced the family room in the old farm house with its 14-foot-high ceiling have been at least a foot taller than the ceiling, causing the star at the top to loop sideways.

Decorating it is a two-day chore, and un-decorating takes an equally protracted time. I take it slowly, one branch at a time.

When it is all done, and the furniture is rearranged, I can truly say that I feel the New Year has arrived.

But this past year there was Wally the clown in a dog suit to contend with and perhaps some of the issues that marked my ill-fated leap from the hay mow.

The holiday season was an endless fascination to His Puppiness, with a seemingly constant stream of new visitors to lick into submission. But it was the Christmas tree that Wally liked the most of all. He would lie underneath it at the base, and stare up its trunk at the sparkling lights and baubles, mesmerized for hours.

When I began chopping the tree down, there was considerable puppy angst.

It would be convenient to be able to remove the Christmas tree neatly in one piece, but with such a large tree it is impossible.

Just getting the tree into the house involves removing windows and pulleys and levers and at least six hands.

Such enthusiasm seldom prevails past the transformation of the turkey carcass into broth, let alone into the early weeks in January.

So I get out my hack saw and gradually whittle the tree into a singular vertical log, removing light strands and ornaments as I go.

I had the first of the bottom branches removed before young Wally realized what was happening. The boughs were scattered on a white sheet beneath the tree that approximates "snow" and helps keep the fallen needles from clogging the vacuum.

At first he was merely bewildered. Then he began to howl. His face was now a mask of sorrow. If I didn't know better, I would have sworn there were tears beneath the triangles where his eyes live. I opened the window beside the tree and hurriedly shoved the branches outside. Immediately, Wally demanded to be let outside.

As he was bounding through a drift of snow, I watched him grab a tinsel-covered branch and drag it steadfastly to a corner of the backyard which he has claimed as his own.

This went on all day long, resulting in a well-worn path speckled with spruce needles. At the end of it there lay a chaos of Christmas tree branches.

In the living room, the trunk of the once bountiful tree was all that remained of Christmas past. Wally whimpered at the base of the ladder when I slipped the star from its lopsided crowning branch. Whined big time when I took what remained of the tree out of the stand and lobbed it javelin-style out the window.

Under normal circumstances the detritus of the stale-dated Christmas tree would be stacked behind the wood pile for future burning or wood chipping. But for now it has new life as the playground for a Snoopy clone.

Wally spends hours rearranging the branches, jumping on them, crawling through them and shaking them vigorously. There is no *auld lang syne* for this tree.

Like the blackened sunflower stalks that still nod heavy-headed in the snow-covered garden, the piecemeal recycling of the old Christmas tree is a small reminder that what goes around, comes around.

Wally doesn't know that yet.

But I can't help thinking that there are only 345 days, give or take a week or two, before we start combing the forest for a new tree and rearranging the furniture for another holiday season.

That's how I start the New Year with a definitive, optimistic vision of its end already in sight. Whoever said "familiarity breeds contempt" must never have lived in the country.

This book was set with Palatino and Galliard fonts.